Inside The Church of Almighty God

Inside The Church of Almighty God

The Most Persecuted Religious Movement in China

MASSIMO INTROVIGNE

OXFORD
UNIVERSITY PRESS

Oxford University Press is a department of the University of Oxford. It furthers
the University's objective of excellence in research, scholarship, and education
by publishing worldwide. Oxford is a registered trade mark of Oxford University
Press in the UK and certain other countries.

Published in the United States of America by Oxford University Press
198 Madison Avenue, New York, NY 10016, United States of America.

© Oxford University Press 2020

All rights reserved. No part of this publication may be reproduced, stored in
a retrieval system, or transmitted, in any form or by any means, without the
prior permission in writing of Oxford University Press, or as expressly permitted
by law, by license, or under terms agreed with the appropriate reproduction
rights organization. Inquiries concerning reproduction outside the scope of the
above should be sent to the Rights Department, Oxford University Press, at the
address above.

You must not circulate this work in any other form
and you must impose this same condition on any acquirer.

CIP data is on file at the Library of Congress
ISBN 978-0-19-008909-2

1 3 5 7 9 8 6 4 2

Printed by Sheridan Books, Inc., United States of America

Contents

Introduction: A Visit to Jeju Island and Other Adventures vii

1. The Suicide of Ms. Liu and Other Chinese Persecution Stories 1
   Liu Limei 1
   Zheng Yang 3
   Jiang Guizhi 4
   Gao Cuiqin 7
   Jiao Fuqun 9
   Nan Xiangming 10
   Zhang Ruixia 11
   Cui Shuya 12
   He Linbo 13

2. China's Struggle against the *Xie Jiao* 16
   Sinicization 16
   Xie Jiao 18

3. The Church of Almighty God: Origins and Beliefs 27
   Origins 27
   The Time of Spiritual Trials 31
   The Man Used by the Holy Spirit 37
   Persecution and Expansion 37
   Basic Beliefs: The Three Ages 42
   The Millennial Kingdom 45

4. Joining The Church of Almighty God 49
   Why the Phenomenal Growth? 49
   Ann 51
   Max 52
   Tina and Charlie 53
   Christopher 54
   The Anti-Cult Perspective 55

CAG Doctrine and the Family	56
Survey Results	62
Conclusion	69

5. Living in The Church of Almighty God ... 70
   - Organization and Demographics ... 70
   - A Minimalist but Rich Worship ... 72
   - A Theology of Beauty ... 74
   - Visual Arts in the Diaspora ... 75

6. Fake News: The McDonald's Murder of 2014 ... 80
   - Academic Studies of Fake News ... 80
   - Enter the Scholars ... 83
   - The McDonald's Case: An Introduction ... 88
   - The Story of a Micro-Movement ... 89
   - The Eve of the Crime: The Sad Story of a Dog ... 94
   - The Murder ... 96
   - Conclusion ... 99

7. The Red Dragon and the Pastors: Accusations of Kidnapping ... 102
   - The Red Dragon Strikes Back ... 102
   - An Evangelical Cliffhanger ... 105
   - But Was the Story True? ... 109
   - Conclusion ... 112

8. Escaping China: The Refugees ... 117
   - An International Crisis ... 117
   - Six Objections ... 119

9. Some Conclusions: The Church of Almighty God in Xi Jinping's China ... 126

References ... 133
Index of Personal Names ... 147

Introduction: A Visit to Jeju Island and Other Adventures

On January 6, 2019, the day of the Epiphany in my own Catholic tradition, I was standing in a large but overcrowded apartment on Jeju Island, South Korea, hosting some forty refugees from a new Chinese religious movement, The Church of Almighty God ("The" is always capitalized). Jeju Island is situated midway between the coast of China and Seoul; a 2018 Korean law mandates that refugees applying for asylum must remain on the island until their application has been resolved. They are not permitted to work, so they spend their days waiting for a decision from a country where obtaining protection is difficult. All of the refugees in the apartment that day had arrived from China in 2018. Only a few of them spoke English. With the help of an interpreter, they told their stories of persecution, separation from their loved ones, and in some cases torture. They were nervous and scared, and many wept profusely. They asked only one thing: that their stories be told to the world.

This book starts by relating stories of Chinese believers who were arrested, detained, and in some cases, tortured and killed because of their faith. All the stories concern members of The Church of Almighty God. While the literature on religious persecution in China often disguises the names of the victims in order to avoid retaliation on their relatives, in the stories I relate in the first chapter all names are real.

But membership in The Church of Almighty God is not the only element these refugees have in common. They are all supported by affidavits sworn and submitted to the United Nations' Human Rights Council in Geneva for the Universal Periodic Review of China in 2018 (with the single exception of the case of Jiang Guizhi, whose affidavit, although duly sworn, did not reach Geneva on time and could not be filed). Every five years, each member state of the United Nations is expected to submit to the Human Rights Council an assessment of its human rights record. Nongovernmental organizations (NGOs) may also present reports on the human rights situation in a country. Those Universal Periodic Reviews submissions found to be admissible are published on the Human Rights Council's website. With respect to the Universal Periodic Review of China, six different submissions mentioned the persecution of The Church of Almighty God. One was cosigned by Coordination des associations et des particuliers pour la liberté de conscience, an NGO enjoying consultative status with the Economic and Social Council of the United Nations.

It is notoriously difficult to prove torture and extrajudicial killings in totalitarian regimes. However, in the case of the members of The Church of Almighty God, China's Universal Periodic Review of 2018 was a turning point. The persecution of church members was mentioned in the Report of the Office of the United Nations High Commissioner for Human Rights, summarizing the submissions received about China (United Nations Human Rights Council 2018). On January 14, 2019, the Tom Lantos Human Rights Commission included for the first time a member of The Church of Almighty God, Ms. Mo Xiufeng, in the list of prisoners of conscience "adopted" by this bipartisan body of the U.S. House of Representatives, created in 2008 to advocate for human rights (U.S. Congress, Tom Lantos Human Rights Commission 2019). Other international documents followed. The U.S. Department of State mentioned in its two 2019 reports on human rights and religious liberty that more than 11,000 members of the Church of Almighty God were arrested in 2018 and hundreds suffered torture in custody (U.S. Department of State 2019a, 4 and 2019b). The U.S. Commission on International Religious Freedom included similar comments in its 2019 report (U.S. Commission on International Religious Freedom 2019, 40). Slowly, an impressive body of evidence is being collected, documenting that the abuses against the devotees of The Church of Almighty God in China are very real. Without being accused of specific crimes, thousands of members of the church have been arrested and sentenced to long terms of detention and forced labor. As I will detail with specific examples, being a member of The Church of Almighty God or simply found in possession of its literature is enough to warrant arrest.

But what is The Church of Almighty God? And why is it persecuted? The Church of Almighty God (CAG), in Chinese Quannengshenjiaohui (全能神教会), is a Chinese Christian religious movement, founded in 1991, also known as Eastern Lightning. The latter name refers to a passage in Matthew 24:27: "For as lightning that comes from the east is visible even in the west, so will be the coming of the Son of Man." This "lightning that comes from the east," according to the church, is Jesus Christ returning as Almighty God, that is, as a person born in China, a country in the East, to inaugurate the third age of humanity.

The persecution of the CAG was started because of its phenomenal growth, which panicked the authorities, and its theology, which teaches that the Chinese Communist Party (CCP) has been consistently "resisting God" and incarnates the evil red dragon of the Book of Revelation. Is the CAG really a threat to the CCP, or is it just another independent Christian movement in China, misunderstood but inoffensive?

In this book I try to answer basic questions about the CAG. As a starting point, I explain how and why certain groups in China are labeled *xie jiao* (邪教, "heterodox teachings") and persecuted. I then present the history, main beliefs, and practices of the CAG, seeking to explain its rapid and surprising growth. I address the Chinese regime's persecution of and media attacks against the CAG and the main criminal accusations, including homicides and kidnappings, raised against this movement. Although some incidents are open to different interpretations, investigations by independent scholars have so far identified such accusations as part of a massive and spectacular campaign of fake news, created by the Chinese regime in order to justify a persecution that was started, for political and ideological reasons, well before the CAG was accused of any crime.

In its campaign against the CAG, the CCP has been supported by Christian groups that see the CAG as a dangerous, heretical group, even a "cult." Its theology is undoubtedly original, although CAG believers claim that their doctrine simply comes from the words of Almighty God, the returning Jesus Christ of the last days, which produced a latter-day sacred scripture. Their point of view should be understood and respected. Most scholars, aware that its theology is certainly different from that of traditional Christian churches, describe the CAG as a Christian new religious movement. The American scholar Holly Folk (2018) believes that the concept of Christianity is continuously developing. She argues that even though the CAG has proposed innovations with respect to traditional Christianity, its theology is ultimately rooted in Protestantism and it has maintained "Protestant continuities" with respect to mainline Christian teachings. She concludes that the CAG should indeed be considered a Christian movement (68).

Like all religious movements, the CAG did not arise in a vacuum. It emerged during the early 1990s revival of Chinese Christianity within a network of house churches whose theology was indebted to both the Reformed and the Brethren traditions. Understanding these roots, and CAG beliefs, is not a purely theological exercise. It is because of both its rapid growth and its theology, which includes criticism of Marxist atheism, that the CAG is perceived as an enemy by the CCP.

This book is mostly based on primary sources and on my interviews in 2017, 2018, and 2019 with members of the church in several countries (South Korea, Taiwan, the United States, Canada, Japan, Australia, Switzerland, Belgium, the Netherlands, Italy, France, Germany, Greece, Finland, Spain, Hungary). It was often not easy for them to share dramatic personal stories, and I want to thank them here for their cooperation and openness. They are all refugees and prefer to remain anonymous. This work is also based on interviews with officers of the Chinese police, anticult activists (including some who claimed to be former members of the CAG), and scholars engaged in the CCP's official campaign against the church. I conducted this set of interviews during two trips to China in 2017. From them, I learned that China now regards the CAG as "the new Falun Gong," in fact a threat more dangerous and massive than Falun Gong. More police officers, I was told, are deployed hunting members of the CAG than are hunting members of Falun Gong, which has been successfully eradicated in several provinces and cities (or so the officers claimed).

The book took its present shape after conversations with colleagues who have also studied the CAG and interviewed CAG refugees in various countries: J. Gordon Melton, Holly Folk, Jim Richardson, Susan Palmer, Bernadette Rigal-Cellard, and Ed Irons. I am grateful to all of them for their comments and insights and for generously sharing unpublished material. I also thank the lawyers and NGO activists representing CAG refugees in various countries who discussed their cases with me, Luca Ciotta of the Center for Studies on New Religions in Torino, Italy, who helped with the Index, and the peer reviewers, editors, and staff at Oxford University Press. Finally, the book reflects a continuous conversation on CAG refugees' issues with Rosita Šorytė, whose long experience as a former diplomat specializing in humanitarian aid has been of invaluable help. Her contribution and constant support for this project goes well beyond technical issues, and this book is dedicated to her.

1
The Suicide of Ms. Liu and Other Chinese Persecution Stories

Liu Limei

On the evening of July 17, 2009, Liu Limei, a medical worker, and her husband were on their way home to the residence community of China National Coal Group, in the city of Shuozhou, in the Chinese province of Shanxi, when they were intercepted by more than a dozen police officers. Liu was arrested, accused of being a member of The Church of Almighty God, a religious movement on the government's list of banned religious groups.

She was taken to the police station and continuously interrogated for two days and three nights. During this time, the police officers did not let Liu sleep and compelled her to remain in a half-squatting position (a stress position frequently used in torture) for a long time. Liu was too weak to resist and collapsed to the ground several times. The interrogations went on for nine days.

She was released on bond but was regularly monitored by police officers. She reported seeing strange cars parked near her house, and that a car would trail her every time she went out. In her workplace, where she was the director of the Emergency Department in her company's medical unit, she often saw suspicious people wandering around outside her office. The police also ordered Liu's managers to put pressure on her, resulting in reprimands from her chiefs and ridicule from her colleagues because of her religious faith. She suffered extreme mental duress, and six months later was forced to resign.

Inside The Church of Almighty God. Massimo Introvigne, Oxford University Press. (2020).
© Oxford University Press.
DOI: 10.1093/oso/9780190089092.001.0001

Ten months after her release from jail, the police installed a camera on the wall of the home of Liu's neighbor, monitoring her constantly. Her house was frequently visited by the police. Informed that she would be arrested again soon, she fled, leaving behind her twelve-year-old daughter and her frail and sick father, and went into hiding for a period. But she could not evade the police for long, and upon her return home she was arrested. Since then her husband has been demoted at work and her son has never been promoted, despite the fact that both are model workers.

Due to the constant and prolonged tension and anxiety, Liu suffered from depression and severe insomnia; once cheerful and extraverted, she became reticent and reserved. Add to this the consequences of police abuse during her arrest, and Liu's mental health and physical condition kept worsening. Two years later, she became so ill she was forced to take sick leave from her new job.

In June 2014, Liu was again warned that she was about to be arrested, and again she fled, hiding in a small house in Shuozhou. The police interrogated her husband many times about her whereabouts and prodded his work managers to put pressure on him, but he did not reveal her hiding place.

Liu did not dare to go out during the day or turn on the lights at night. Despite his fear that he would lead the police to her, Liu's husband continued to visit her, taking taxis at night to bring her food and other necessities, each time staying for no more than two hours.

Faced with the threat of a new arrest, surveillance, and harassment, Liu could not stand the tremendous mental pressure. She became extremely thin and had problems swallowing food. Eventually, on November 16, 2014, Liu committed suicide by jumping into a river in Lüliang, Shanxi (Human Rights without Frontiers 2018b).

Zheng Yang

On December 7, 2012, Zheng Yang of Xinmi, in the Chinese province of Henan, was identified as a member of the CAG. He was arrested by the police, who shackled his hands and feet and took him to an interrogation room. There they hit the tops of his feet with an iron bar five or six times, while he hung by his hands from an electric fan on the ceiling. This torture was repeated three times and lasted about twenty minutes.

After he was taken to a detention center, police officers repeatedly suspended him using the handcuffs, beat him, and incited other prisoners to beat and torment him. Sentenced to three years in jail for having been active in a banned religious organization, Zheng was compelled to perform backbreaking manual labor every day, was not allowed to wear shoes in winter, and was forced to bathe in cold water, while the prison guards hit him on the head with heavy electric batons.

Like all those who had been arrested as members of a banned religion, Zheng was forced to write a monthly "thought report" to show how his "reeducation" was progressing. In early 2015 he wrote in his thought report, "All positive things come from God, and all negative things come from Satan." This enraged the instructor of the division, who beat Zheng on the head and back with high-voltage electric batons until Zheng was trembling and going numb from head to toe, started to be delirious, and collapsed. After that, the guards arranged for two other prisoners to keep watch over him around the clock. Zheng tried to commit suicide and was confined to a tiny four-square-meter room for a month, where he started to experience hallucinations and trance-like states.

Having finally completed his sentence, he was released, but suffered from amnesia. He stared at others blankly, refused to eat and drink, and urinated and defecated in his bed. After forty days of this behavior, he was sent to Fusheng Psychiatric Hospital in

Xinmi, where he was diagnosed with schizophrenia, a condition, he was told, he had first developed a year earlier. With treatment, he has shown some improvement, but he appears dull, frightened, and timid. As of 2018 he still required daily medications (Omnium des Libertés and Canaan Human Rights 2018).

Jiang Guizhi

On January 4, 2013, Jiang Guizhi was arrested by the police for being a member of the CAG. Jiang lived in the city of Zhumadian, Henan, where she was a leader of her religious community.

At around 1:00 p.m. Jiang arrived for a religious assembly at the rented apartment of a sixty-three-year-old woman surnamed Zheng, located at the southeastern corner of Qingping Square in the city of Xinmi, Henan. Shortly after 7:00, eight police officers, headed by Yu Hongchao, the captain of the Xinmi National Security Brigade, burst into the room. According to Zheng's account, the police did not present any official documents before apprehending her, Jiang Guizhi, and another woman, Zhang Li. Jiang and Zhang were put in handcuffs.

The police ransacked the apartment; not even the toilet trash was spared. They used a knife to slice open the sofa cushions, looking for anything hidden inside. They seized religious books, RMB 10,000 (about $1,400) in cash, computers, mobile phones, items of clothing—even household goods, cooking utensils, and food.

That same evening, at around 9:00, Jiang and the other two women were taken to the Xinmi Public Security Bureau. Two days later, on January 6, Captain Yu and several police officers escorted Jiang and Zhang to the Xiyuan Hotel in Xinmi for interrogation. It is common practice in China to take someone in custody for interrogation first to a hotel, although this form of extrajudicial detention is theoretically illegal under Chinese law. From then on, the two women never saw each other again.

A coreligionist who was arrested and detained with Jiang reported that, to force her to provide information about the leaders and members of the CAG, the officers deprived her of sleep for several days: as soon as she closed her eyes, they would kick and punch her. The police also forced her to take off all her clothes and insulted her with profanities. They did not let her use the toilet, forcing her to wet herself. They then made her lick the urine off the ground. Another female coreligionist, also detained at the Xiyuan Hotel, reported that the officers forced her to spread her legs and kneel on a wooden baton. They used a belt to beat her about the face and head, in addition to hoisting one of her legs into the air on a metal frame, leaving her to balance on tiptoe with her other leg. In another method of torture, called "the grilled lamb," she was handcuffed with her arms around her legs, a metal pipe was threaded behind her knees, and she was then hung upside down. The various methods the Chinese police used against these women are an indication of the kind of torture Jiang might have suffered.

After being secretly interrogated for twenty-one days, Jiang was sent to the Zhengzhou No. 2 Detention Center on January 25. Another coreligionist, who was held in the same cell as Jiang and talked to her, reported that after arriving at cell no. 7, Jiang was silent and apathetic. Sometimes she sighed and wept. Her condition worsened rapidly. Several days later she dropped her bowl while eating and was unable to pick it up despite several attempts. One morning several days after that, Jiang was unable to get out of bed. She seemed confused, and her reactions were slow. The prisoner in charge of their cell, Chen Lin, sent several prisoners to force her to get up. She did not know how to dress herself, was incapable of holding a food bowl, and gradually became incontinent. Only when repeatedly asked by her cellmate did Jiang reveal that the police had taken her to a private room in the hotel where she was interrogated, then raped her and stuffed objects inside her vagina. After talking for a short while, she fell silent and became unresponsive. The only way to get her to drink was to spoon-feed her soy milk. Seeing that

Jiang was unwell, prison officers called several prisoners to carry her out on a stretcher. That was the last time her cellmate saw her.

According to the police, Jiang died in the early morning of February 12, 2013, eighteen days after arriving at the Zhengzhou No. 2 Detention Center. Her family was given no information about what had happened to her until February 14, when the local police station in Zhumadian sent an officer to inform them of her death. The family was told that Jiang had died of a heart attack at the detention center.

When Jiang's family saw her body at the mortuary of the Fourth Affiliated Hospital of Zhengzhou University, they were overcome with grief and indignation. A doctor told them that, when she was brought to the hospital, Jiang was foaming at the mouth, was disoriented, and had lost control of her bowel and bladder movements. On her death certificate were question marks written next to recorded symptoms of high blood pressure, heart disease, and cerebral infarction; cause of death was multiple organ failure. Seeing the death certificate confirmed to the family that the police's claim that she had died of a heart attack was an attempt to cover up the truth and avoid responsibility.

In their search for evidence, Jiang's family asked to see the records of her interrogation. The police firmly refused, but did allow them to watch surveillance videos of Jiang's day-to-day life in the detention center. The recordings showed her to be in very poor physical condition during the last days of her life. When she tried to drink water, it dribbled from her mouth. She was incapable of dressing herself and unsteady when using the toilet, needing help to pull her trousers up. When Jiang's family asked the police why they had not immediately taken her to the hospital, given how evidently serious her condition was, they claimed they had not realized she was ill. When her family asked why she had been arrested, Bai Shuangfeng, who had been in charge of handling the case at the Xinmi Public Security Bureau, replied that Jiang had been arrested because she was a member and a leader of a banned religious group.

Afterward the Zhengzhou police made several trips to Pingyu County to threaten Jiang's family. They also ordered officials from the local county Communist Party committee and county government, as well as the managers of the workplaces where Jiang's brothers-in-law and son worked, to put pressure on the family to keep the case secret. They threatened to monitor their phone calls, asserting that the family would suffer the consequences if they talked about the case. In the end, Jiang's family had no choice but to stop pursuing the matter any further.

On March 5, 2013, Jiang's body was cremated at the Zhengzhou Crematorium. On March 9 her ashes were brought back to her hometown in Pingyu County and buried in a tomb at Baimiao on the east side of the crematorium (Li 2018).

Gao Cuiqin

In the early morning of July 15, 2014, around 6:30, Gao Cuiqin, a farmer living near Zibo City, Shandong, was at home making breakfast when six plainclothes police officers (four male and two female), led by Gong Yuebing, deputy captain of the Shandong Huantai County Public Security Bureau National Security Brigade, burst into her family home. Gao's mother-in-law and sister-in-law were standing in the home's entrance at the time; they watched as the officers accused Gao of being a member of the CAG and forced her to accompany them to the local Public Security Bureau station. After registering her, she was transferred to the Huantai County Detention Center. Around noon that same day, the police returned to Gao's home and demanded that her mother-in-law pay for Gao's living expenses while detained. She refused.

Emergency personnel at Huantai County Shengjie Hospital later disclosed that around 11:00 a.m. on July 17 the police called the hospital requesting an ambulance for a medical emergency. A doctor rushed to the detention center, but he concluded that Gao had already been dead for some time and saw no reason to bring her body to the hospital. The police made another phone call, this time to the Huantai County branch of the Shandong Qilu Hospital, whose emergency personnel agreed to retrieve Gao's body.

At 1:00 p.m. that day, Zhao Xuepeng, the director of the Suo Town Police Station in Huantai County, called Gao's husband, Mr. Liu, told him that his wife was in the hospital, and urged him to go there; he did not mention that she was already dead. About an hour later, Gao's sister-in-law and brother-in-law went to the hospital, but they did not find her there, nor did the hospital have a record of her hospitalization. At 6:00 that evening, Gao's husband met with the police and inquired into his wife's condition but received no clear answer. He was taken to the hospital, where he saw two tubes in his wife's nose and a flat line on the ECG. Her head was twisted at an angle and her neck was tilted up; her body was stiff. It was clear that she had been dead for a while, but the doctor was still using an external pacemaker, pretending he was trying to save her. Liu overheard another doctor say that his wife had shown no signs of life when she arrived at the hospital. Liu took a photo of his wife's body and showed it to an emergency department staff member, who admitted that Gao had been dead for some time when she was brought to the hospital, and that she showed clear signs of having been brutally beaten. Her entire face was purple and extremely swollen.

Another CAG member, who was held in the same detention center as Gao, later reported that around 5:00 a.m. on July 16, she had heard sounds of a beating from the adjacent room, where Gao was being interrogated. She believed she was hearing the impact of iron shackles hitting a body and horrifying screams. After that, everything went silent. Yet another CAG member, detained at that time at the Suo Town Police Station, overheard a phone call by an officer reporting that an inmate had died at the detention center after being repeatedly hit with a taser. She later realized the inmate was Gao.

In the afternoon of July 18, when Gao's family were at the funeral home taking care of her remains, they found several red marks on her back; her face was blue, and her head was twisted to one side. They simply could not straighten it out. A longtime employee of the Public Security Bureau later confirmed to the relatives that Gao's injuries were consistent with her being tied to a chair and tased at very high voltage.

Gao's family demanded to see video recordings of her interrogation, but the police refused. They claimed Gao had a preexisting heart condition, which led her to death from sudden cardiac arrest. Her family denies she had such medical history (Center for Studies on Freedom of Religion Belief and Conscience and Association for the Defense of Human Rights and Religious Freedom 2018).

Jiao Fuqun

On July 24, 2014, Jiao Fuqun was arrested in the basement of the house of his friend Nan Xiangming, in Junma Township, in the city of Xianyang, Liquan County, Shaanxi. He was sentenced to one-year imprisonment in the Liquan Detention Center in Xianyang, from July 25, 2014 to July 24, 2015, for being a member of a banned religious group.

Police officers beat Jiao, cuffed his hands behind his back, and kicked and stamped on his body with their leather shoes. They beat his ankles with a wooden stick so severely that the stick broke in two. One policeman then drilled the splintered stick into Jiao's calf. The pain made him scream out loudly, and beads of sweat rolled down his face.

The police officer paid no attention to Jiao's bleeding calf and continued to ruthlessly beat his ankles for forty more minutes. Other officers placed several bricks under his cuffed hands on his back, then stepped on him and fiercely lifted the handcuffs on, driving the metal into his flesh. Jiao's arms were full of pain and felt as though they were being torn from his body. After more than an hour, a police officer finally unlocked the handcuffs, fearing that their prisoner might die; it took several minutes to pry the metal out of the skin around his right wrist, and Jiao fainted from pain. Two officers dragged him to the faucet and poured cold water over his head and wounds, waking him. His bruised hands and one wrist were dripping blood and his right foot was so swollen that he could not stand up.

On the second day, July 25, the police took him directly to Liquan County Detention Center. There a guard punched him in the face and chest and incited the other inmates to beat him. For months, Jiao suffered continuous abuse in prison. He was forced to squat for long periods and to work for thirteen hours a day, which prevented the wound on his right leg from healing. He endured severe pain as his wounds became inflamed and discharged. He still bears the consequences of the abuses (Soteria International and Association on Study of Religion and Human Rights 2018).

Nan Xiangming

Nan Xiangming, in whose home Jiao Fuqun had been found by the police, was also arrested on July 24, 2014, and jailed for being a member of the CAG. On August 2 Nan and the others arrested with him, wearing prison uniforms and handcuffed and shackled, were escorted to the village where Nan lived and paraded in public. Later the seventy-three-year-old was transferred to Weinan Prison, Shaanxi, to serve his three-year sentence. Three days after he arrived there, the prison authorities called his daughter and asked her to pay for the drugs to treat Nan's diabetes. His family were not allowed to visit or to send him anything, including medicine; they could only make monthly payments to his bank card.

On February 1, 2016, the prison once again called Nan's daughter and asked her to send RMB 20,000 (about $2,900) for his health care expenses. The next day the daughter went to the prison and learned that he was in critical condition and had been sent to a prison hospital in Xi'an, Shaanxi.

When she found him in the hospital, Nan managed to tell his daughter that the long period spent in prison without enough to eat had resulted in a deterioration of his diabetes. When he did eat, he vomited, and his throat was always sore. His daughter's successive requests for her father to be released from custody and transferred to a regular hospital for treatment were rejected.

At 9:00 p.m. on February 7, 2016, Nan's family received a call from the prison. The authorities said that all measures had proved ineffectual and that Nan had died. In fact, diabetic syndrome triggered by high blood sugar had led to coronary heart disease. The family maintains that he was deliberately not treated for diabetes because of his religious beliefs (Soteria International and Association on Study of Religion and Human Rights 2018).

Zhang Ruixia

On June 25, 2014, the farmer Zhang Ruixia was arrested in the city of Linzhou, Henan, for being a member of a proscribed religious group. Her family asked the village cadre many times where Zhang was detained but received no answer. Finally, in January 2015, a member of the same religious movement told Zhang's family that she had been seen handcuffed to a tiger bench in the Public Security Bureau; it was obvious she had been beaten. "Tiger benches" are benches to which victims of torture are tightly tied using belts, with bricks or other hard objects placed under their feet to increase pressure. Later the family learned from another Christian arrested at the same time that Zhang had been killed.

Zhang's brother, together with other five people, including the village cadre himself, went to the State Security Brigade of Linzhou, where they were allowed to see her remains. The brother later testified, "Zhang Ruixia was a plump person, but when I went into the morgue, I saw her skinny remains. She often worked in the field and her feet were big, but they were turned to smaller ones, like a teenager's. There was a long sewn-up slit down the abdomen, which looked empty, with the internal organs pulled out and removed. Her remains were not recognizable, and only the jaw and teeth showed that she might be Zhang. The body was later identified as Zhang through a DNA test."

When Zhang's brother and her son asked how she died and why the police did not notify them of her death, they were told that she got sick and died of natural causes. Her family and friends did not believe this. In March 2015 over twenty people, including members of Zhang's family and neighbors, went to the Public Security Bureau to demand justice for Zhang; they carried banners protesting her arrest and treatment. The police confiscated the banners, beat Zhang's younger sister and nephew, and told the protesters to go home immediately or they would be arrested.

Zhang's family wanted to bring her remains home, but the authorities refused, telling them that her body would be cremated (Coordination des associations et des particuliers pour la liberté de conscience et al. 2018).

Cui Shuya

On June 19, 2015, Cui Shuya was arrested in Beijing as a member of the CAG and taken to a police station in the Daxin District. To extract information about his banned religious organization, police officers dragged Cui to the toilet, where they slapped him fiercely on his face and delivered a heavy blow to his chest. One police officer hit his hands and teeth with an electrified baton. Cui's mouth was pried open and pepper spray was forced into it. He felt as though he were suffocating, and snot and tears poured out of his nose and eyes.

He was thrown to the floor and stripped of his pants, and an officer applied electric shocks to his legs, chest, and private parts. Cui felt as if his private parts were being penetrated by a long nail, and he cried aloud. A police officer stepped on his head, and another kicked his mouth. His private parts were shocked again and he smelled burning flesh.

On another day, the police sprayed pepper water into his nostrils, and blisters later appeared on his face. He was pulled outside, and a police dog was sent to attack him. Then the police officers took him back to the interrogation room and demanded that he renounce his faith. When he refused, they bound him by his wrists and ankles to an iron chair and left him for the night. Still Cui resisted. For a month he suffered all sorts of abuse before being released, when officials admonished that any attempt to practice his faith would lead to another arrest (Omnium des Libertés and Canaan Human Rights 2018).

He Linbo

On the morning of November 26, 2017, He Linbo was arrested at the Shihezi City Train Station in the Xinjiang Uyghur Autonomous Region. He was accused of being a local leader of the CAG and was escorted to the police post of the train station, where he was searched and beaten.

At noon on the same day, he was confined in the Shihezi City Detention Center. There the head prisoner, a prisoner appointed by the jail to oversee the others, ordered him to mop the floor and toilet. The head prisoner forced him to strip naked and squat in the toilet, with both hands on his head, then poured basin after basin of cold water over his head. This was during the coldest days of the winter. He was shivering from the cold while suffering from a terrible headache, but the head prisoner ordered him to shout that the water was in fact not cold, and stopped pouring it only after He complied.

On November 27, He was taken to the Guangming Road Police Station in Wujiaqu City, Xinjiang, for interrogation. The police handcuffed him to a tiger bench and prevented him from sleeping for several days. Four officers stood guard. At one point the State Security Brigade captain twisted an electric wire into a cable as thick as a finger and took turns with three others, including the Criminal Police Squad captain, whipping He's back, chest, and legs. The captain then whipped him with a thinner copper wire. Handcuffed to the tiger bench, He was unable to avoid the brutal beating. Later the agents whipped him on his hands and, removing his shoes, whipped the tops and bottoms of his feet. The pain made him scream.

Because He was not answering their questions, the captain delivered him over to four younger policemen, who took him down from the tiger bench and fed him mustard oil. They made him do half-squats for twenty minutes, repeated three times with a ten-minute break in between. His face was covered with sweat and his legs were trembling uncontrollably. Afterward the police handcuffed him to the tiger bench again.

The next day the police escorted him to the Sixth Agricultural Division Detention Center in Wujiaqu City. During a strip search, he saw that his body was covered with wounds, his legs were bruised, and his feet were so swollen that he could not put on shoes. On December 11 he was transferred to a hotel room in Wujiaqu City for a "secret interrogation," as often happens in China. There the police handcuffed him to a tiger bench and deprived him of sleep for seven days and nights. As soon as he dozed off, the police opened the window to let in the freezing cold and rubbed his head, face, and neck with towels soaked in cold water. Wearing only a thin cotton T-shirt and a pair of pants, he was trembling all over.

After dinner on the evening of December 17, sitting on an iron chair with his hands cuffed, He found he could withdraw his hands from the metal rings, and he started looking for a chance to escape. The two police officers watching him that evening relaxed their guard, believing he was too weak to escape. One of them went to sleep, and after the other forced He to read aloud the report of the Nineteenth National Congress of the CCP while the officer played with his cell phone on the bed, he too fell asleep. He Linbo then slipped out of the handcuffs, put on the clothes and shoes the police had hung in the closet, and left the room. As the holidays were approaching, the entrance doors of the hotel were not locked, and the entrance guard was sleeping on the sofa. He Linbo escaped from the hotel and reached the home of a coreligionist, where he found temporary shelter. At the time of this writing, he is still at large (Center for Studies on Freedom of Religion Belief and Conscience and Association for the Defense of Human Rights and Religious Freedom 2018).

2
China's Struggle against the *Xie Jiao*

Sinicization

At first sight, the cruel persecution of the CAG in China may appear irrational, for, as mentioned earlier, it does not find a justification in the crimes allegedly committed by the CAG. The accusations of crimes committed by members of the CAG are largely created by Chinese propaganda, spread to justify the persecution after the fact. The CAG was already being persecuted for many years when the first accusations of crimes emerged, proof that the crimes were not the cause of the persecution.

The persecution is not justified by the fear of the Chinese regime that the CAG may instigate a revolution against it. In fact, the idea that the CAG may be both willing and able to organize a revolution against the Chinese government verges on the ridiculous. And the Chinese authorities understand that the virulence of the persecution against the CAG tarnishes their international image, something they take quite seriously.

To understand the behavior of the Chinese regime, I introduce two concepts: sinicization and *xie jiao*. Both are often misunderstood in the West. By placing them within the Chinese context, the reasons why the regime cannot tolerate non-sinicized religions and *xie jiao* will become clear.

The word "sinicization" existed before the Communist regime took power, long before its present application to religion. The concept, if not the name, dates to the Middle Ages (Elliott 2001). It originally referred to policies introduced by Beijing authorities to persuade and, if necessary, compel non-Han ethnic and linguistic

Inside The Church of Almighty God. Massimo Introvigne, Oxford University Press. (2020).
© Oxford University Press.
DOI: 10.1093/oso/9780190089092.001.0001

minorities, such as the Miao or Uyghurs, to adopt Chinese culture, language, and customs.

In the nineteenth century, commercial enterprises managed by Westerners started to appear in China, as well as Christian churches led by foreign missionaries. The word "sinicization" was used in late Imperial and republican China to indicate a marked hostility against organizations operating in China but directed by foreigners, be they entrepreneurs, humanitarian activists, or missionaries. "Sinicizing" an organization meant putting it under Chinese leadership.

The CCP inherited the word and used it quite liberally, but with a different meaning. To be regarded as "sinicized," it was now not enough for an organization to have Chinese leaders; those leaders had to be appointed by the government or the CCP, and the organization had to operate within the framework of the aims and principles defined by the CCP. President Xi himself has clarified that the sinicization of religions means that they should strictly follow the leadership and directives of the CCP, operate "under the Party," and follow its "active guidance" (Li 2017). Religious organizations born in China and directed by Chinese are not regarded as sinicized if they are not fully integrated into the CCP-dominated Chinese system.

The Chinese system for controlling religion, as it developed after the Cultural Revolution (1966–76) and after the so-called *Document 19* of 1982 (Central Committee of the Chinese Communist Party 1982), which recognized that religion in China would likely not disappear in the foreseeable future, thus distinguishes between two, or more correctly three, categories of religions. The first category includes the *fully sinicized religions*, strictly following the CCP's instructions; they are allowed to operate publicly under the control of and with leaders appointed by the CCP and include the Three Self Church (a body established in 1954 that, according to the government, should include all Protestant churches in one single organization) and the Chinese

Patriotic Catholic Association. These organizations are not monolithic, and their local pastors and priests may have very different degrees of loyalty to the regime, but certainly their core leadership is strictly controlled by the CCP (Vala 2018; see also Reny 2018). The second category includes the *non-sinicized religions*. In this group are the Underground Catholic Church, loyal to the Vatican (although it is expected that it will gradually merge with the Chinese Patriotic Catholic Association as a result of the 2018 deal signed between China and the Holy See), and the flourishing Protestant "house churches," which exist precariously and can be hit by the regime at any time. The New Regulation on Religious Affairs, which was signed into law on August 26, 2017, and came into force on February 1, 2018, increased the pressure on the house churches to merge into the Three Self Church and stop operating independently. Those who would not comply were threatened with the destruction of their places of worship and the arrest of their leaders (Li 2017).

In fact, however, there are three rather than two categories in the Chinese system of religions. In 2006 the sociologist Yang Fenggang distinguished between the "red market" of the sinicized religion in China and the "gray market" of those non-sinicized. But he also indicated the existence of a third, "black market," including the groups labeled "*xie jiao*." All movements identified as *xie jiao* are non-sinicized, but not all non-sinicized groups are regarded by the regime as *xie jiao* (Yang 2006, 2012).

Xie Jiao

The expression *xie jiao* is translated in Chinese official documents into English as "cults" or "evil cults." The translation, however, is inaccurate and is connected to an attempt to argue that the problem of "cults" is not only Chinese but international. In fact, the notion of *xie jiao* was born in the Ming period, and a more correct translation is "heterodox teachings." The Ming preoccupation with *xie jiao* was rooted in a century-old tradition of Chinese millenarian movements trying to take over the government. While some of them posed very real threats to the empire, others were outlawed based on a variety of political and religious considerations (ter Haar 1992). What teachings were heterodox was determined by the emperor, and lists of *xie jiao* were constructed on both theological and political grounds. For example, Christianity as a whole was classified as a *xie jiao* in 1725 but taken off the list in 1842 due to Western political and military pressure (Goossaert and Palmer 2011, 27–31).

The republican and Communist governments inherited this old notion and policy. The category of *xie jiao* was used both in Taiwan, during the Martial Law period, and in Mainland China in the 1950s for the now forgotten massive persecution of Yiguandao, a large Chinese non-Christian new religious movement, which in fact became the model for the subsequent repression of other groups. According to police reports, in the campaign against *xie jiao* of 1953–54, largely directed against Yiguandao, 820,000 "leaders and organizers" and 13 million followers were arrested or otherwise persecuted (Shao 1997, 452, 455).

"*Xie jiao*," however, was not the main term used during these campaigns. The CCP preferred to define the persecuted groups as "reactionary secret societies" (*fandong huidaomen*) or "feudal secret societies" (*fengjian huidaomen*), labels that reflected Mao Zedong's belief that some secret societies had played a progressive rather than a reactionary role in Chinese history (Palmer 2012). *Huidaomen* was used to emphasize that banned groups, although they might use the mask of religion, were not really religious, were similar to organized crime, and remained outside the area of religious liberty theoretically guaranteed by the Chinese Constitution.

"*Xie jiao*" came back as the favored term in the 1990s. The Hong Kong scholars David Alexander Palmer (2012) and Edward Irons (2018) believe that a return to the prevalence of the label "*xie jiao*," which was again preferred to "*huidaomen*," was determined by the CCP's attempt to elicit the sympathy of both Westerners opposed to "cults" and the mainline Christian churches, which feared the competition of Christian new religious movements they regarded as heretical. At times the label "cult" was used by the CCP in a cavalier way and applied to all forms of religion not authorized by the Party. However, a systematic theory of the *xie jiao* as "evil cults," a translation, as mentioned earlier, adopted by the Chinese regime itself but in fact less accurate than "heterodox teachings," emerged only with the incidents of the late 1990s that persuaded the CCP that Falun Gong was a dangerous competitor and enemy (Irons 2018, 41).

This generated the inclusion of a new crime, "using" a *xie jiao*, in the Chinese Criminal Code in 1997, the creation of a special State Security unit called Office 610 (from the date of its establishment, June 10, 1999) for dealing with the *xie jiao*, and the establishment throughout China, and in some centers of the Chinese diaspora abroad, of branches of a Chinese Anti-Xie-Jiao Association (called in English Chinese Anti-Cult Association), directly connected with the CCP (Irons 2018, 41). In March 2018 it was announced that the Central Office 610 was being discontinued (while its local branches continued to exist), its functions absorbed into the CCP Central Political and Legal Affairs Commission as well as the Ministry of Public Security (Irons 2019).

When these measures came into effect, the old practice of compiling official lists of *xie jiao* had already been revived, with the first national list published in 1995. The list included both Christian new religious movements such as the Shouters, the CAG, the Association of Disciples, and the Full Scope Church (also known as the All Sphere Church, Word of Life Church, or the Born-Again Movement), and non-Christian groups, including the True Buddha School and the movement founded in Taiwan by the Vietnamese meditation master Ching Hai. Falun Gong was added to the list in 1999 (Irons 2018, 44).

Article 300 of the Chinese Criminal Code made using a *xie jiao* a crime punishable with jail sentences from three to seven years or more (Permanent Mission of the People's Republic of China to the United Nations and Other International Organizations in Vienna n.d.; this translation does not include the 2015 amendments). It is important to determine what "using a *xie jiao*" means exactly within the context of Article 300, which was amended in 2015. Not all decisions of the Chinese courts are published online, but thousands of them are. And there is a vast number of published decisions in which members of a *xie jiao*, particularly of the CAG (listed as a *xie jiao* since 1995), were sentenced to long periods in jail (often exceeding seven years) based on Article 300. It is clear from hundreds of decisions that "using a *xie jiao*" is interpreted as being active in a *xie jiao* in any capacity. Although leaders receive harsher punishments, it is by no means necessary to be a leader to be recognized as guilty of having used a *xie jiao* under Article 300. In fact, both being found in possession of literature of the CAG and trying to convert others to the Almighty God faith have been regarded as sufficient evidence of guilt of the crime punished by Article 300 (see, e.g., China Judgements Online 2014, 2017; Introvigne, Richardson, and Šorytė 2019).

Monetary rewards are offered in China to those who supply the police with names of members of *xie jiao*, including the CAG, and information leading to their arrest. Again, higher rewards are offered for the leaders, but rewards are also paid to those who denounce a simple devotee. Some of the rewards tables were posted on the internet by the relevant Chinese authorities and local media (see Pingtan County 2015; Shandong Anti-Cult Association 2017).

That *xie jiao* are illegal and are regarded by CCP as a black market of religions that includes the most dangerous non-sinicized organizations, is abundantly clear. Much less clear is the definition of *xie jiao*. In 2000 a confidential document by the Chinese Ministry of Public Security stated that a group should be regarded as *xie jiao* if it

a. establishes an illegal organization in the name of religion, *qigong*, etc.;
b. deifies its leaders;
c. initiates and spreads superstitions and heterodox beliefs;
d. utilizes various means to fabricate and spread superstitions and heterodox beliefs to excite doubts and deceive the people, and recruit and control its members by various means;
e. engages in disturbing social order in an organized manner that brings injury to the lives and properties of the citizens. (Irons 2018, 34)

Such definitions are obviously quite vague. The most recent attempt to date of improving this one while incorporating its criteria resulted in Rule 1 of the *Interpretations on the Issues concerning the Application of Laws in Criminal Cases relating to Organizing and Utilizing Evil Organizations to Destroy Law Enforcement*, issued on January 25, 2017, by the People's Supreme Court and the Supreme People's Procuratorate. *Xie jiao* were defined as "illegal organizations, which, through fraudulent use of religion, *qi gong*, or any other name, by deifying and promoting their ringleaders, or by fabricating and spreading superstitious fallacies and other means to confuse and deceive others . . . control group members and harm society" (Supreme People's Procuratorate of the People's Republic of China 2017).

In practice, such broad definitions mean that groups that are regarded as *xie jiao* are simply those that are included in the lists of *xie jiao* periodically updated by the Chinese authorities. To be included in the list, it is not necessary for a group to be accused of specific crimes. Promoting teachings the CCP regards as "superstitious" or hostile to the Party is enough. The CAG has consistently been included in all lists of *xie jiao* published since 1995 (Irons 2018). Indeed, with the reduction of the activities of Falun Gong in Mainland China, the CAG has emerged in recent years as the main target of anti-xie-jiao policies, and in all provinces it seems that special branches of Office 610 (or their successor structures) are now devoted exclusively to fighting the CAG (Zoccatelli 2018, 5).

But problems of definition remain. The Chinese Anti-Xie-Jiao Association continues to cooperate with American and European anti-cult organizations and individuals (Chen 2017; Xu 2017). However, thanks in particular to the pioneering efforts of the American scholar of new religious movements J. Gordon Melton, at least some of the Association's leaders gradually came to realize that the notion of "cult" they had tried to borrow from American and European anti-cultists was widely criticized by Western academics. Adopting it as a definition of *xie jiao* would therefore not defuse the international criticism of what many see as the Chinese repression of religious liberty.

This, and the fact that scholars who do not share the anti-cult approach were invited to China, does not mean that Chinese authorities are ready to introduce a new definition of *xie jiao*. But it appears that they are open to discussion.

There are different approaches to the *xie jiao* question within the CCP itself. Three Self pastors, who are sometimes close to the CCP, are supported by a venerable tradition when they insist that *xie jiao* should be defined as heretical groups that deny the basic truths of traditional religions. The Party's Marxism notwithstanding, they believe they can persuade the CCP that the only antidote to bad religion is good religion. This notion presupposes that it is possible to define "bad religion." Since Christian or post-Christian groups such as the CAG are now prominent in the Chinese *xie jiao* discourse, the proposed standard is the Protestant version of the Bible. "Unbiblical" groups are to be considered *xie jiao*. Pastors are less competent when it comes to criticizing non-Christian groups such as Falun Gong, but they may claim, analogically, that these represent heretical distortions of the Three Teachings (Buddhism, Confucianism, and Taoism).

It is somewhat paradoxical that an officially irreligious state may seriously consider deciding which religious groups should be repressed based on criteria such as the nature of Jesus Christ or the traditional doctrine of the Trinity. Yet there are those in the CCP who believe that, while religion will eventually disappear in the distant future, for the time being the best way of eradicating *xie jiao* is to promote pro-governmental Christianity in the shape of the Three Self churches and rely on the propaganda of their pastors (see Palmer 2012).

A second approach, which is represented by several Chinese academics, most of them members of the CCP who specialize in the study and criticism of *xie jiao*, maintains that "cults" are a universal problem, not a Chinese problem only. Some academics were busy promoting translations of standard American and European anti-cult works and even invited deprogrammers to China (Chen 2017; Xu 2017). They eventually realized, however, that this approach had the disadvantage of creating extremely long lists of *xie jiao*, while the CCP and the police would prefer to concentrate their resources on the few groups that develop most rapidly. They regard the rapid growth of certain religious movements as dangerous for the Party. Hence the translation of *xie jiao* as "destructive cults," a term also used by Western anti-cultists, or (more commonly) as "evil cults," with the implication that not all "cults" are truly destructive or evil.

Some Chinese academics imported from Western anti-cultism the notion of brainwashing as the distinctive character of "destructive cults." This was another paradox, since the very word "brainwashing" was originally coined by American intelligence during the Cold War to support anti-Chinese propaganda. Brainwashing was something the evil Chinese Communists did (Anthony 1996; Anthony and Introvigne 2006). Chinese courts, including the People's Supreme Court, stayed away from brainwashing controversies and, as mentioned earlier, described *xie jiao* as groups spreading "superstition," which is defined as something opposed to both science and socialism, and different from genuine religion. In fact *xie jiao* are also defined as "pseudo-religious" movements (Chen 2017).

As Melton (2018) points out, it is important to emphasize that for the CCP and the Chinese courts *xie jiao* are not religions. Therefore any Western objection about religious liberty is dismissed as irrelevant. Chinese authorities would answer that religious liberty is guaranteed by the Chinese Constitution, but *xie jiao* have nothing to do with religion.

This is an old attitude, and not only a Chinese one. Usually those hostile to "cults," when confronted with the objection that the repression of "cults" violates religious liberty, respond that "cults" are not religions. This was the position of the anti-cult camp in the "cult wars" of the late twentieth century (Richardson 1978, 1979, 1993; Introvigne 2014; Gallagher 2016). But the position dates back to at least one century before the cult wars. It is difficult to deny that in nineteenth-century America Catholics were discriminated against and persecuted, even though the patriotic narrative portrayed the United States as a country whose very origins were rooted in the affirmation of religious liberty. Anti-Catholic crusaders such as Charles P. Chiniquy, a former Canadian Catholic priest turned Presbyterian minister, insisted that Catholicism was not a religion but a subversive political organization, a business empire, or a criminal racket promoting immorality (Davis 1960). It was only by asserting that Catholicism was not really a religion that the image of the United States as the country of religious freedom could be reconciled with the reality of anti-Catholic discrimination.

However, in nineteenth-century America this was merely a rhetoric device, as it is in contemporary China for *xie jiao*. Who decides that one religion is genuine and another only pretends to be a religion? Often, as the sociologist Larry Greil claimed in 1996, "religion" is "not . . . a characteristic which inheres in certain phenomena, but . . . a cultural resource over which competing interest groups may vie" (48). And the competition, in different ways in democratic compared to totalitarian societies, is settled not by science but by power. In twenty-first-century China, the motto of the imperial Roman jurist of the second and third century A.D., Ulpianus, still resonates: "Quod principi placuit, legis habet vigorem" (What pleases the emperor becomes enforceable law). The CCP, the new emperor, now decides which groups are *xie jiao*. They are taken out of the sphere of religious liberty and human rights and their members are dehumanized. In fact, according to the CCP's own proclamation, *xie jiao* should be "totally eradicated like tumors." Tumors have no rights, and can only be eradicated through violence.

3
The Church of Almighty God
Origins and Beliefs

Origins

The first scholarly accounts of the CAG, which were based on parts of its earlier books and websites rather than on personal interaction with members, stated that its devotees were reluctant to discuss the origins of their movement (Dunn 2015, 47–49). My interviews, which of course refer to later years with respect to these early studies, would lead to the opposite conclusion. I found CAG members happy, even eager to share the story of their origins. In 2018 they even opened a permanent exhibition about their origins and history in their main church in Seoul (see The Church of Almighty God 2019a). Scholars visiting Seoul during international conferences were contacted and invited to visit the exhibition, and the same happened for some journalists. The story as told by CAG members is, understandably, narrated from an insider's perspective. It does supply some mundane elements, such as dates and places, but mostly it insists on sacred, theological features.

As one of my interviewees put it, "Jehovah God issued the laws that initiated the Age of Law and generated Judaism. Two thousand years ago, Jesus Christ performed the work of redemption that initiated the Age of Grace and generated Christianity. Undoubtedly, The Church of Almighty God came into existence entirely because of the appearance and work of Almighty God and absolutely was not established by any human." CAG members like to draw a parallel with the origins of Judaism and Christianity,

Inside The Church of Almighty God. Massimo Introvigne, Oxford University Press. (2020).
© Oxford University Press.
DOI: 10.1093/oso/9780190089092.001.0001

as recorded in their respective holy scriptures. Both claim they came into existence because of the work of God. Similarly, they argue, the CAG was born as a result of the utterances, appearance, and work of Almighty God. "At the beginning," another interviewee told me, "many people from various denominations of Christianity heard the voice of Almighty God, and they saw that the words of Almighty God unlocked many mysteries in the Bible and that He expressed all the truth to purify and save mankind, so they confirmed that the Lord had come back and they accepted Almighty God."

Deng Xiaoping came to power in China in 1978. The so-called Reform and Opening-Up period followed in the 1980s, generating inter alia a revival of religion and an unexpected, large development of Christian house churches. Among the latter, a noticeable growth was experienced by those in the tradition (known as "the Local Church" in the West) of Watchman Nee (Ni Shu-tsu), a Chinese Christian leader who in the 1930s was influenced by a branch of the Exclusive Brethren, a fundamentalist Christian denomination, although he later separated from them, and of his gifted co-worker Witness Lee (Li Changshou). Some of the house churches in this tradition were referred to in China as "the Shouters" (from their practice of invoking the name of the Lord in a loud voice; Introvigne 2018g, 83–85).

These developments alarmed the CCP. The Shouters were identified as a *xie jiao* in 1983 and included in the 1995 *xie jiao* list. Other house churches were also severely persecuted. As often happens in times of persecution, millenarian expectations also emerged. In the words of one of my interviewees, who lived through these years and later joined the CAG, "Among the house churches in various places, especially in the Local Church [the Shouters], Christians who truly believed in the Lord, though suffering persecution, still continued to assemble and read the Bible, pray to the Lord Jesus, and expect him to return soon to save them from the darkness. It was among these house churches that

Almighty God appeared and began to work and utter His words." He added, "Almighty God first appeared to work and expressed truths amongst believers who were part of the Shouters, but the CAG theology is not associated with the Shouters."

Several scholars believe that the CAG identifies the incarnated Almighty God with a Chinese woman, Yang Xiangbin, who was born in 1973 in northwestern China (Dunn 2015, 68–72). However, the movement never mentions the name nor any biographical details of Almighty God and refuses to confirm details supplied by outside sources. They explain this choice as "a form of reverence for God." Almighty God is also constantly referred to as "he" rather than "she" by CAG members, although they believe that in the last days God was incarnated as a woman. The CAG's main holy scripture, *The Word Appears in the Flesh*, states, "Back then, when Jesus came, He was male, but when God comes this time, He is female" (The Church of Almighty God 2017e, 899).

The person identified by the CAG as Almighty God formally entered the house church movement in 1989 and began to utter words on February 11, 1991, that followers later compared for authority and power to those expressed by Jesus Christ. These utterances transmitted a message to all the nations: "God has already come into the human world, God is going to initiate an even greater work, God's kingdom has already descended into a certain group of people" (The Church of Almighty God 2018c). Several Christians in the Chinese house church movement believed that those words were from the Holy Spirit and carried authority and power like those of Jesus, and they started reading these messages in their gatherings in the same year, 1991.

Zhao Weishan (b. 1951), a native of the Heilongjiang province in China, was at that time the leader of several communities of the Shouters. He took the lead in accepting the messages and the work of Almighty God and spread them throughout house church believers. In February 1991 Zhao received the messages in northeastern China and arranged for copies to be distributed to house churches he led in that region and sent to other provinces, such as Henan, Shanxi, and Anhui.

One of my interviewees who witnessed the events of 1991 reported, "These words showed people the path of practice for entry into life and unlocked many mysteries in the Bible, which fulfills the prophecy of the Lord Jesus: 'I have yet many things to say to you, but you cannot bear them now. However, when He, the Spirit of truth, is come, He will guide you into all truth' [John 16:12–13]. God's chosen people were attracted by God's words and confirmed in their hearts that these words were the Holy Spirit's words to the churches as prophesied in the Book of Revelation and were the scroll opened by the Lamb."

On May 8, 1991, Zhao barely escaped arrest during a meeting in Heilongjiang. He moved to Henan and asked the person who was uttering the messages to come to Henan as well. From then on, the utterances multiplied. For security reasons, they could not be published, so instead they were typed by the early CAG members, copied, bound into booklets, and sent from Henan to other provinces. The person later recognized as Almighty God, in the meantime, moved around Henan, staying in Kaifeng, Changyuan, Anyang, Dengfeng, Pingdingshan, Yexian County, and elsewhere. The city of Kaifeng was later identified by the Chinese police as "the central nexus" of the CAG (The Church of Almighty God 2019a).

What was so unique in these utterances that inspired so many to believe in them and risk their life and liberty to spread them? Several of my interviewees pointed to the same passage in *The Word Appears in the Flesh* as containing special significance; these words persuaded them that, while Jesus had performed the work of salvation, only the new revelation of Almighty God could eradicate human corruption. The passage is worth quoting in its entirety:

> In the last days, Christ uses a variety of truths to teach man, expose the essence of man, and dissect his words and deeds. These words comprise various truths, such as man's duty, how man

should obey God, how man should be loyal to God, how man ought to live out the normal humanity, as well as the wisdom and the disposition of God, and so on. These words are all directed at the essence of man and his corrupt disposition. In particular, those words that expose how man spurns God are spoken in regard to how man is an embodiment of Satan and an enemy force against God. In undertaking His work of judgment, God does not simply make clear the nature of man with just a few words; He exposes, deals with, and prunes over the long term. These methods of exposure, dealing, and pruning cannot be substituted with ordinary words, but with the truth that man does not possess at all. Only methods of this kind are deemed judgment; only through judgment of this kind can man be subdued and thoroughly convinced into submission to God, and moreover gain true knowledge of God. What the work of judgment brings about is man's understanding of the true face of God and the truth about his own rebelliousness. The work of judgment allows man to gain much understanding of the will of God, of the purpose of God's work, and of the mysteries that are incomprehensible to him. It also allows man to recognize and know his corrupt substance and the roots of his corruption, as well as to discover the ugliness of man. These effects are all brought about by the work of judgment, for the substance of this work is actually the work of opening up the truth, the way, and the life of God to all those who have faith in Him. This work is the work of judgment done by God. (The Church of Almighty God 2017e, 1408–9)

The Time of Spiritual Trials

From February to September 1991 the utterances included more than 100,000 words. One interviewee remembered, "Each day, God's chosen people were watered and provided for by God's words. They came to know and understand some truths and mysteries and saw the path of practice for entry into life, feeling that they had gained a lot. Their hearts were completely conquered by the words of Almighty God and confirmed that believing in Almighty God would ensure their entering the kingdom of heaven and receiving rewards, promises, and blessings from God."

In October 1991, however, the utterances acquired a different tone, indicating, as they now recall, that the first believers were "[seeking] to gain God's rewards more than God himself." The person speaking as Almighty God now revealed, "In China, apart from My firstborn sons and My people, all the others are the offspring of the great red dragon and are to be discarded" (The Church of Almighty God 2019b). Apart from a small number of "firstborn sons," the other believers were "service-doers" who were seeking God's rewards instead of seeking God himself. They were "offspring of the great red dragon," who will render service to the cause of God for a while and then will "be destroyed into nothingness." Hearing these new messages, the young community went from euphoria to despair. "God's chosen people" (as CAG members refer to themselves) believed they had endured much suffering for God and certainly did not expect to be regarded as mere "service-doers" doomed to perish. After going through a painful trial and reading again Almighty God's words, one interviewee explained, they understood they were indeed originally "the offspring of the great red dragon and the ilk of Satan, and that they were unqualified to enter the kingdom of heaven and gain God's inheritance." But "it was by God's exceptional uplifting and grace that they had the opportunity to hear God's utterance, enjoy God's supply of life, and be able to do service for the supreme God. Realizing that, the chosen people of God came out from their negativity and abandoned much of their motivation to be blessed. They were willing to render service for God and obey his orchestrations and arrangements."

Five months later, on February 20, 1992, a message from Almighty God revealed that these had indeed been months of trial and that the "service-doers" had become the "people of the kingdom."

According to the CAG, the trial of service-doers was the first step that God undertook to purify the chosen ones. It was the first of the "the six initial trials of the work of judgment beginning with the house of God." This period constitutes an essential part of the CAG's sacred history. (I have reconstructed it through interviews with Brother Xing Dao, Sister Xin Rui, and Sister Cheng Xin, in Seoul in October 2018; all three were part of the first group of believers who accepted the messages of Almighty God in 1991, and quotes in this chapter come from their interviews unless otherwise specified; see also The Church of Almighty God 2019a).

The second of these six trials was the "trial of death," which lasted from March 1992 to May 15, 1992. Regarding themselves as the "people of the kingdom," CAG members had believed they would not die and would soon enter the Kingdom of Heaven alive. Almighty God's utterances, however, exposed this belief as false. Members learned that human flesh was filled with satanic dispositions and was under the power of Satan and thus doomed to die. They felt the weight and agony of these words in their heart, as their delusions of entering the Kingdom of Heaven alive were torn apart. Once again they were plunged into what my interviewees described as a "refinement." By reading Almighty God's word and studying it in their assemblies and fellowships, they realized that the "trial of death" was intended to "break their extravagant desires," "make them know God's holy and righteous disposition," teach them that corrupted human beings are not allowed to enter the Kingdom of Heaven before being purified and saved by God, and ask them to put their lives entirely at the mercy of God, allowing God to fully purify them.

What followed was the third trial, "the time of loving God," from May 15, 1992, to February 1993. Although believers were willing to lay aside their fleshly hopes for the future and had resolved to follow

God until the end of their lives, they didn't yet know how to do so but simply obeyed passively. As one of the interviewees described it, "They were not active in their understanding of God's intention. The majority of God's chosen people did not understand what it meant to love God. They thought loving God was difficult and were clueless about how to love God. It was under these circumstances that God required people to love him." The utterances described the impurity and wrong intentions that members' love for God often contained and taught them what love for God really is and how to put this love into practice. The messages revealed God's love and plan of salvation for humanity and explained that loving God for the rest of one's life would make life meaningful. Having learned the true way to love God, many set their new understanding in prayer, resolving to love God regardless of the blessings or misfortunes they received. They participated more actively in the church's work. Some gave up their jobs and devoted themselves to the church as full-time workers.

Continuing the work of purification, as the early members I interviewed recalled, Almighty God carried out "the trial of the foils" (fourth trial, February–May 1993) and the "trial of the Descendants of Moab" (fifth trial, May–November 1993; the name comes from Genesis 19:37). These trials further corrected members' wrong perspectives about faith in God and their own corrupt disposition.

The sixth trial, the "trial of the great red dragon's offspring" (1996–97), was described to me as "the primary and central work of Almighty God's judgment in the last days." Almighty God revealed that "God's chosen people in China" (i.e., CAG members) were offspring of the dragon and had been poisoned by the dragon. More than one hundred poisons of the great red dragon had materialized in lifestyles and folk wisdom, expressed in popular sayings such as "I am my own Lord throughout heaven and earth" and "Everyone for himself and the devil takes the hindmost." These popular Chinese tenets had made the people arrogant, deceitful, and selfish and caused them to "resist God increasingly." The CAG believes that, by undergoing this sixth trial, devotees were able to know the origin of their sins and became willing to dispel the effects of the great red dragon's poisons and put into practice God's truths for their purification. According to my interviewees, they believe that only at the end of the six trials did they experience true repentance, achieve some changes in their corrupt disposition, and understand that God's judgement and chastisement are true salvation and love.

The six trials ended in 1997, but as one of my interviewees put it, "of course, people can't be completely purified by only experiencing these six trials. They will still receive similar trials later in their experience. . . . Even for God's chosen people who accept his work after 1997, they will also experience trials like these until they get rid of their corrupt disposition."

The trials are both sacred metaphors and historical events in the life of the community. Although they were painful, the CAG believes that they were needed in order to purify members of arrogance, deceitfulness, selfishness, and other "satanic" dispositions and correct false ideas that had contaminated their faith in God. The trials allowed "God's chosen people" to see that they had been "deeply corrupted by Satan" and needed to undergo Almighty God's work of chastisement and purification to get rid of their corruption and gain God's salvation.

In the CAG's reconstruction of its sacred history, Almighty God's work has fulfilled the prophecy in the Bible, "For the time has come that judgment must begin at the house of God" (1 Peter 4:17). This "work of judgement" also reveals the outcome and destination of each class of humans. In Almighty God's own words, "When God becomes flesh this time, His work is to express His disposition, primarily through chastisement and judgment. Using this as the foundation, He brings more truth to man, shows more ways of practice, and so achieves His objective of conquering man and saving man from his corrupt disposition. This is what lies behind the work of God in the Age of Kingdom" (The Church of Almighty God 2017e, vii). "When His work ends, those people who remain will be cleansed and enjoy a more wonderful second human life upon the earth as they enter a higher realm of humanity; in other words, they will enter into humanity's day of rest and live together with God. After those who cannot remain have undergone chastisement and judgment, their original forms will be entirely revealed; after this they will all be destroyed and, like Satan, will no longer be allowed to survive upon the earth" (The Church of Almighty God 2017e, 1368).

It can be said that this "work of judgement" performed by Almighty God is the core teaching of the CAG. It is also interpreted as evidence that Almighty God is really incarnate in our time, because only God can purify, change, and save humanity.

From February 1991 to the end of 1992 Almighty God had uttered more than one million words that CAG members accepted as the words of the Holy Spirit. However, they did not yet realize that God had become flesh. They regarded the person they would later recognize as Almighty God as performing a special function, as a prophet conveying the words of God. Not until the end of 1992, when Almighty God revealed the mystery of incarnation and explained the essential difference between the incarnate God and prophets and other human beings used by God, did "God's chosen ones" recognize that the person who expressed these words of truth and worked among them was God incarnate and Christ who had appeared again to work on Earth.

In 1995, having experienced Almighty God's words and work for several years, CAG members realized, as one interviewee reported, "God's eager intention to save mankind in the last days, so they had the burden to spread the gospel and began to testify about God's appearance and work of the last days to various [Christian] denominations." A large missionary work thus began.

The Man Used by the Holy Spirit

The messages from Almighty God also named Zhao Weishan as the Man Used by the Holy Spirit and the Priest of the CAG, and he was unanimously recognized by the community as such. Zhao's role thus was founded in the very words of Almighty God. The CAG is personally led and shepherded by Almighty God incarnate, while Zhao is cooperating with the work of Almighty God and is in charge of the administrative affairs of the church. His role is compared by the CAG to that of Moses in the Age of Law and Peter's in the Age of Grace.

Some Chinese sources refer to Zhao as the founder of the CAG. However, some scholars believe this is due to reluctance to admit that a woman may be the founder of a large religious movement and that, while Zhao's role is certainly important, the actual founder of the CAG is the (female) person it recognizes as Almighty God (CESNUR 2017).

Persecution and Expansion

The message that Jesus had returned filled the believers of the new community with great enthusiasm and evangelistic zeal. From 1995 on, they announced the new gospel to Christians of all denominations all over China, starting with the house churches. From 1997 to 1999 the CAG spread rapidly in Henan, Shandong, northeastern China, Hebei, Shanxi, Shaanxi, Anhui, and Jiangsu, converting a significant number of house church believers. In 2002 the missionary work extended to China's southern provinces, border areas, and ethnic minority regions By 2005 CAG communities had spread across the whole of Mainland China, with a total membership around one million.

Entire local communities of denominations and movements joined the CAG; these included the Shouters, Sola Fide (Justification by Faith), the Born-Again Movement (also known as Full Scope or All Sphere Church), the Three Grades of Servants, the Association of Disciples (Mentuhui), the True Jesus Church, the Spirit Church (also known as Efficacious Spirit Teachings, Linglingjiao), and the Seventh-day Adventist Church. In some large denominations and movements, half or more of the members accepted the message of the CAG. The same happened, according to my interviewees, with communities of the Roman Catholic Church. The figures cannot be confirmed independently, but house churches and Three Self pastors I interviewed in China regard them as believable. In its early years the CAG grew mainly by converting large portions of local communities of other Christian denominations. This both alarmed the CCP, causing increasing persecution, and angered rival religionists, who reacted with a strongly worded indictment of the CAG, claiming that conversions were obtained through deceptive strategies. These opponents spread various rumors, denounced the CAG to the authorities, and in some cases resorted to actual physical violence (Dunn 2015, 47).

It was a time of deep hostility and bitter reactions from other Christian groups, as my interviewees recalled. One stated, "They [other Christian denominations and movements] aggressively accused the CAG of stealing their sheep. They even called the police and cooperated with the CCP to arrest the believers of the CAG. Many believers of the CAG, when spreading the gospel to the religious world, were reported to the police and beaten. Some were forced to disappear because of spreading the gospel to them." Another interviewee explained, "The leaders of various denominations hated the CAG so much because the words of Almighty God are the truth and carry authority and power, from which people from various denominations heard the voice of God and turned to Almighty God. The reason why leaders in the religious world harbored bitter envy and intense hatred was probably that this threatened their positions and their livelihoods. As a result, they flew into a rage and devoted their efforts to creating ridiculous lies and rumors that opposed and condemned Almighty God's work of the last days." A sister who was there in these years concurred: "They [leaders of other Christian churches] also spread the rumors and false accusations created by the CCP against the CAG. They had the churches sealed off and tried to prevent people from seeking and investigating the true way. They even verbally and physically assaulted the CAG believers testifying about God's appearance and work of the last days, and reported them to the police for arrest. This is the same as what the Pharisees did when the gospel of the Lord Jesus spread to Judaism. They were afraid that the believers of Judaism would turn to the Lord Jesus and forsake Judaism so that they would lose their positions and livelihoods. That's why they hated the Lord Jesus so much, fabricating many rumors and even nailing him on the cross."

In the mid-1990s a harsh repression targeted several house churches and Christian movements, including the Shouters and the Born-Again Movement. As mentioned earlier, several Christian groups, including the CAG, were formally banned as a *xie jiao* in 1995 and have been severely persecuted ever since. On August 7, 2000, the Chinese Ministry of Public Security held a closed-door meeting in Tai'an City of Shandong Province, during which it claimed that the CAG was growing at an alarming rate and demanded that "The Church of Almighty God Project" be set up. Codenamed "Project 807," it provided a unified command within national borders to carry out special investigations and suppression of the CAG. Bi Rongsheng (2001), deputy director of the Religion Section of the Department Public Security of Hebei Province, delivered a speech at a Project 807 coordination meeting on September 14, 2000. His speech was analyzed in 2002, and declared genuine, by Freedom House, which also published and discussed another five CCP confidential documents on the crackdown on the CAG (Center for Religious Freedom 2002).

In 2000 Zhao, who had been hunted by the CCP for many years, fled to United States and in 2001 was granted political asylum there.

According to Chinese government sources, the person the CAG worships as Almighty God also escaped to the United States during that time and currently lives there. This information, as any other concerning the person of Almighty God, is not confirmed (nor denied) by the CAG. One leader I interviewed in Seoul put it this way: "The whereabouts of Almighty God are not important. What is important is that he is with us, utters words of truth, and personally leads and shepherds the church." Since then, the movement has been directed from New York.

In early 2009 He Zhexun, who used to be in charge of the work of the church in Mainland China, was arrested by the Chinese authorities and sentenced to fifteen years in prison. He remains in jail to this day. On July 17, 2009, Ma Suoping, who took over He's role, was also arrested by the Chinese police, this time in Tangshan, Hebei. She was transferred to Zhengzhou, Henan, and on July 24 her family was informed that she had died of a heart attack. Her husband and daughter reported that her body, which they saw in the morgue of Zhengzhou's Yellow River Central Hospital, was covered in bruises and scars; they did not believe that Ma had died of natural causes (Human Rights without Frontiers 2018a, 42).

The numbers of persecuted are impressive. The CAG itself reports that between 2011 and the end of 2017, at least 400,000 members were arrested by the Chinese authorities, and another 11,000 in 2018 alone, with frequent instances of torture and 101 cases of death since the church's foundation, 20 of them in 2018, either in jail or as a consequence of police abuse (The Church of Almighty God 2019c). Several refugees I interviewed told me of frequent violence they had suffered while in jail, as CAG members were compelled to wear special insignia on their prison uniforms. The convicts who tormented them were not punished, and were even encouraged to continue. Such reports and figures are impossible to confirm when dealing with totalitarian regimes. However, I find them not unbelievable, considering how often Chinese media report that several dozen or even several hundred CAG members have been arrested in one or another province or city. When I attended two anti-CAG seminars in China in 2017 and mentioned the church's figures, I was told by high-ranking police officers that the number of those arrested is confidential. But I was *not* told that the CAG's figures were exaggerated or absurd.

Despite the government's repression and the hostility by some leaders of mainline Christian churches, the CAG continued its growth in China and, according to some Chinese official sources, reached four million members in 2014 (Ma 2014). Since the Zhaoyuan McDonald's murder of 2014 (to which we will return shortly), the repression in China has intensified, and several thousand members have escaped abroad, where they have founded churches in South Korea, Japan, the Philippines, New Zealand, the United States, Australia, Canada, and Europe, in addition to those established in Hong Kong and Taiwan. Non-Chinese started joining the CAG in South Korea, the United States, and elsewhere. Although ethnic Chinese still form the majority of the communities in most diaspora countries, my own observation found as many as 30% of non-Chinese members in some of the overseas communities.

Although it was persecution that led to the CAG's expansion overseas, members see behind this globalization process the work of the Holy Spirit and God's guidance. As one of my interviewees put it, "The kingdom gospel of the Almighty God has spread all over the world, and this exactly fulfills the Lord Jesus's prophecy: 'For as the lightning comes out of the east, and shines even to the west; so shall also the coming of the Son of man be' [Matthew 24:27]. This is not simply due to the persecution and the diaspora, but because God does his work in a way of establishing a model and then broadening it, and ultimately it will spread across the entire universe, just as the Lord Jesus first worked in Judea and then his work spread to the whole world. The work of Almighty God will surely spread to every country in the world."

Basic Beliefs: The Three Ages

The Word Appears in the Flesh, first published at the end of 1993, is a collection of the utterances of Almighty God, amounting to more than one million words, including "what the Spirit saith unto the churches" (Revelation 2:7, 11, 17; 3:13) and the truths to be expressed by "the Spirit of truth" (John 16:13) in the last days, as prophesied in the Bible (see The Church of Almighty God 2017e).

Folk wrote in 2018 in her study of CAG theology, "The CAG does not disavow the Bible, though it is often accused of doing so. The Bible is recognized as the scripture of the Age of Law and Age of Grace" (62). Recorded by human beings, the Bible "contains messages from God and some truthful insights, which are helpful to know God's work in the Age of Law and the Age of Grace, but it also carries many human errors" (62). Almighty God warns, "Not everything in the Bible is a record of the words personally spoken by God. The Bible simply documents the previous two stages of God's work, of which one part is a record of the predictions of the prophets, and one part is the experiences and knowledge written by people used by God throughout the ages" (The Church of Almighty God 2017e, 829–30). While the errors in the Bible should be identified by relying on Almighty God's teachings, the Old and the New Testament also contains genuine messages from God, which are still valid in the Age of Kingdom.

The CAG defines as a member whoever truly believes in God, has "good humanity" (*ren xing*, 人性, a traditional concept in China), and is certain that Almighty God is the returned Lord Jesus. According to the church, China is the place where the Second Coming of Jesus Christ, the "Eastern Lightning," must manifest himself and is the first stop of God's work in the last days.

The church's interpretation of the great red dragon, an evil figure mentioned in the Book of Revelation, is often addressed when discussing the CAG and is one of the reasons why the church was persecuted in China (Dunn 2008a, 2008b). But the church's teaching here may be easily misunderstood. The CAG believes that the CCP has always been "resisting God" and cruelly arresting and persecuting Christians, that it is an evil organization, and that what the CCP does proves that it is indeed the evil great red dragon of the Book of Revelation. As Dunn (2008a) notes, this interpretation of the great red dragon is not unique to the CAG but is found in other Christian churches, including some in the tradition of the Little Flock and the Shouters. The CAG also teaches that the dragon will fall by itself under the weight of its errors, as prophesied in the Book of Revelation. The CAG does not suggest or advocate any uprising or revolution in China, and in fact requires that its members not participate in any political activity. Leaving to God the solution of the dragon problem is consistent with the Christian tradition the CAG is part of.

Almighty God came to inaugurate the third age of humanity, the Age of Kingdom, which follows the Age of Law, the time of the Old Testament, and the Age of Grace, which lasted from Jesus's inauguration of his ministry to the advent and work of Almighty God in the twentieth century.

The Age of Law lasted four thousand years, from humankind's fall (which occurred six thousand years ago, according to the traditional interpretation of the Bible) to when Jesus of Nazareth began his work of salvation. During this period, God revealed himself as Jehovah, gave to the Israelites his Ten Commandments, and led their lives on Earth. Although the sinful nature of humans justified God's wrath, from the expulsion of Adam and Eve from the Garden of Eden to the Flood and beyond, God also revealed and manifested his love.

The Age of Grace was inaugurated by the beginning of Jesus's ministry. Before then, Jesus lived as a human. His divinity was made manifest only after he formally started his ministry. With Jesus's sacrifice on the cross, the sins of humans were forgiven, but their sinful nature was not eradicated. It is for this reason, the CAG believes, that Jesus promised he would come back. One of my interviewees explained, "In the Age of Kingdom, on the basis of the Lord Jesus's redemptive work, Almighty God expresses the truth to do the judgment work, which will thoroughly save humankind from sin, from Satan's fooling and corruption, and purify and make them perfect." As summarized by Folk (2018, 65), "The crucifixion of Jesus accomplished the Redemption work. It also provided new possibilities for humanity to relate to God. Jesus is understood to have redeemed humankind from sin, but he didn't perform the work of removing the sinful nature of humanity." In the words of Almighty God:

> Fully saving man from the influence of Satan not only required Jesus to take on the sins of man as the sin offering, but also required God to do greater work to completely rid man of his disposition, which has been corrupted by Satan. And so, after man was forgiven his sins, God has returned to flesh to lead man into the new age, and begun the work of chastisement and judgment, and this work has brought man into a higher realm. All those who submit under His dominion shall enjoy higher truth and receive greater blessings. They shall truly live in the light, and shall gain the truth, the way, and the life. . . . Although Jesus was able to endure every hardship, to be humble and hidden, to be crucified for God, God only gained one part of His glory, and His glory was gained in Israel. God still has another part of glory: coming to earth to actually work and make perfect a group of people. (The Church of Almighty God 2017e, v; 2015)

In the Age of Kingdom, God becomes flesh in China and achieves the other part of his glory (see The Church of Almighty God 2018e). This work is final, and there will not be another incarnation of God after the present Almighty God. In the last days, the main aim of the work of Almighty God is to eradicate humans' sinful nature (Folk 2018, 61). When a group of believers will have been made perfect, and the righteous will have been acknowledged and the evildoers exposed, the work of Almighty God will come to an end and God and humans will enter into eternal rest.

The Millennial Kingdom

In the theology of the CAG, the Age of Kingdom should not be confused with the Age of the Millennial Kingdom. We are currently living in the Age of Kingdom; the Millennial Kingdom has yet to officially arrive. "During the stage of making people perfect, the Millennial Kingdom is but a fledgling; at the time of the Millennial Kingdom spoken of by God, man will have been made perfect" (The Church of Almighty God 2015). The formula "The Millennial Kingdom Has Arrived" is used by the CAG but described as a "prophecy," which is "analogous to the foretelling of a prophet, one in which God prophesies what will happen in the future."

In the Age of Kingdom, Almighty God speaks "to make people perfect, to purify that which is dirty within them, and to make them holy, and righteous before God." During this necessary purification period, the Millennial Kingdom, as a fledgling, lives as a prophecy in the heart of the believers who are being made perfect and purified by the words of God. Until the Age of Millennial Kingdom is realized, God's glorification on Earth is not yet complete. Only "when the day comes on which people are made perfect by God, and are able to surrender before Him, and can completely obey God, and leave their prospects and fate in the hands of God, then the second part of God's glory will have been entirely gained" (The Church of Almighty God 2017e, 646).

The CAG does not believe Almighty God incarnate will live on Earth forever. After Almighty God returns to "God's dwelling place in Zion" (a location that remains unspecified but does not seem to be on this planet), the disasters prophesied in the Book of Revelation will follow, in the shape of earthquakes, wars, famines, and so on. Planet Earth, however, will not be destroyed. It will become the eternal home of God's purified followers. Almighty God promises, "I will not annihilate the entire world, nor will I annihilate the whole of mankind. I will keep that remaining third—the third that loves Me and has been thoroughly conquered by Me, and I will cause this third to be fruitful and multiply on earth just as the Israelites did under the law, nourishing them with copious sheep and cattle and all the riches of earth" (The Church of Almighty God 2018d).

The great disasters are prophesied in the Bible, but we do not know their details nor their exact dates. Almighty God does not announce the end of the world, but its transformation. And the great disasters will not occur before the work of Almighty God on Earth is completed.

In the Age of the Millennial Kingdom, "people will have already been made perfect and the corrupt disposition within them will have been made pure. At that time, the words spoken by God will guide people step by step, and reveal all of the mysteries of God's work from the time of creation until today, and His words will tell people of God's actions in every age and every day, how He guides people inside, the work He does in the spiritual realm, and will tell them of the dynamics of the spiritual realm" (The Church of Almighty God 2015). The visible sign that the Age of Millennial Kingdom has arrived will be that "all nations will come under God's name, and all come to read God's words," a situation obviously not yet realized in the present Age of Kingdom. With their sinful nature truly eradicated, the "saints" made perfect by God will live forever in the Kingdom, surrounded by peace and beauty (The Church of Almighty God 2015).

As Almighty God revealed, "Throughout the universe, My chosen people live in My glory, blessed beyond compare, not as people living among people, but as people living with God.... This life, this beauty, from time immemorial and forevermore, will not change. This is life in the kingdom" (The Church of Almighty God 2017e, 92). The CAG believes that this millennial scenario will fulfill the prophecy in the Book of Revelation (22:3–5), "And there shall be no more curse: but the throne of God and of the Lamb shall be in it; and his servants shall serve him: And they shall see his face; and his name shall be in their foreheads. And there shall be no night there; and they need no candle, neither light of the sun; for the Lord God giveth them light: and they shall reign for ever and ever." This will be the outcome of God's "six-thousand-year management plan": a new heaven and a new Earth, where those truly purified will live forever.

Dunn (2016) has speculated on the fate of the persons of "good humanity" who are not believers in the CAG (or died before it was established), another difficult subject in the church's theology. She has further speculated on how CAG eschatology may evolve in the future, an exercise that is necessarily largely conjectural (Dunn 2018). Dunn's interpretation of CAG theology is that righteous people of past generations have been, or are being, "reborn" to have the opportunity to gain salvation today. My understanding is that most CAG believers would simply say that God is righteous and will somehow take care of the persons who didn't convert to the CAG; as long as they did not oppose or condemn Almighty God, they will certainly receive God's mercy and grace to survive. Nevertheless, there will be different statuses in the Millennial Kingdom: some will belong to "God's people," and some will be "service-doers" who will be placed under the leadership of God's people. As *The World Appears in the Flesh* explains, "Those who have stood against Me will all perish; as for those whose deeds on the earth have not involved Me, they will, because of how they have acquitted themselves, continue to exist on the earth under the governance of My sons and My people" (The Church of Almighty God 2017e, 95).

Summarizing this eschatology, one could state that the CAG teaches that Jesus Christ, while offering salvation from our sins, did not eradicate the sinful nature of humans. This is the work of Almighty God in our time. When the work of the incarnate God on Earth is finished, and Almighty God departs, after the catastrophes prophesied in the Book of Revelation those purified by God will live forever on an Earth transformed into a millennial kingdom of happiness and peace.

4
Joining The Church of Almighty God

Why the Phenomenal Growth?

As mentioned earlier, it is impossible to assess the number of CAG members in China in any reliable way. Reporters, government agencies, and scholars have cited CAG membership in the tens of thousands to the millions but have rarely provided a rationale for their figure. The Chinese authorities suggest there are between three and four million members of the church (see, e.g., Ma 2014). While these figures may be inflated to justify the need for harsh repression, Chinese police and intelligence departments are among the only agencies equipped to collect data on banned religious groups in China, and their opinion should not be dismissed lightly.

At any rate, there is little doubt that, in the short span between its origins in 1991 and the second decade of the twenty-first century, CAG's growth has been phenomenal. What explains it?

As used in cultural anthropology and religious studies, the term "emic" indicates the insider perspective of the members of a group, that is, how members perceive themselves and interpret their history. In contrast, the term "etic" designates the outsider point of view of observers and scholars (Harris 1983). When explaining the growth of a religion, the emic perspective of the members and the etic point of view of scholars are usually different. Members believe that their religion grew because of divine guidance and its roots in divine truth. Scholars deal with the "human side of religion" (Stark and Finke 2000) and look for more mundane factors. However, sociologists such as Rodney Stark and Roger Finke note that emic and etic explanations are different but not opposed. It would be wrong for social scientists to dismiss doctrine as irrelevant, for in fact the persuasiveness of doctrine is often the key factor for the growth of a religion (Stark and Finke 2000, 257–58).

The emic perspective of the CAG is that it originated from God's work and developed under the guidance of Almighty God's words. Members insist that converts joined the CAG because they came to believe, through reading Almighty God's words, that Almighty God is the returned Lord Jesus, the only true God, who appears in the last days, and that the rapid growth of the church fully demonstrates the authority and power of God's word. They argue that it is because of their special persuasiveness that Almighty God's words resonate with many people. In one of my interviews, a female CAG member insisted that these words "have uncovered all the mysteries held within the Bible and delivered all truths necessary for the purification and salvation of mankind, thus enabling people to have a true understanding of the work and disposition of God, to be cleansed of their corrupted disposition, and to attain God's salvation." The doctrine of the CAG, expressed in its holy scripture, *The Word Appears in the Flesh*, is thus seen as the basis of the church's development and success.

Following Stark and Finke, we need not dismiss these claims as merely theological and, as such, indemonstrable. On the contrary, the two American sociologists maintain that, to grow, a new religion should offer persuasive conceptions of an "active supernatural" agent, who takes care of humanity (Stark and Finke 2000, 258). The CAG proclaims that Jesus Christ has returned to Earth as Almighty God and has initiated the work of "judgment [that] begins with the house of God" and has expressed words to completely purify and save humanity and bring it to a beautiful destination. Obviously, Almighty God's words are persuasive for thousands of converts to the CAG and are a crucial factor in its growth. However, this should not prevent the etic perspective of scholars from looking for other factors that may also play a role in the growth of the church, although the emic point of view of the brothers and sisters of the CAG regards the persuasiveness of the doctrine as perfectly sufficient to explain the church's progress. I will illustrate the emic perspective with the stories of four converts.

Ann

Ann (2017), an American convert, was raised as a Jehovah's Witness. She explains, "Through the years, I saw that the disasters across the world became ever more frequent and the people increasingly panicked and corrupt. In light of the great disasters and various signs of the last days mentioned in Revelation, I was more convinced in my heart that the last days have arrived, and the little scroll [of Revelation 10:10] shall have been opened now. But how is it opened?" Ann did not find persuasive answers among the Jehovah's Witnesses, so she joined a Pentecostal church. There, when she asked for details about the Last Days, the pastor answered, "These are all mysteries, and you don't have to know." Disappointed again, she returned to the Jehovah's Witnesses. But she also wrote of her doubts on Facebook.

Danny, a member of the CAG, responded, "God has come to do His work on earth and expressed the words to judge and purify man in the last days. I know a sister who has more knowledge of God's work of the last days. If you like, I can invite her to have a meeting and fellowship with us about it as well as how the little scroll prophesied in Revelation is opened." Interestingly, and following a pattern repeated in other stories of conversions by Westerners, fellowshipping with the more experienced believer, Sister Flora, also took place on Facebook. She persuaded Ann that "*The Word Appears in the Flesh* expressed by Almighty God in the last days is precisely the little scroll opened by the Lamb mentioned in the Bible" and that it includes the truths that we need to gain purification and salvation in the Last Days.

After reading and "carefully investigating" the words of Almighty God, Ann converted. "I've fully ascertained that Almighty God is really the return of the Lord Jesus. He has opened the scroll and revealed all the mysteries. Then I lost not a moment in preaching the gospel to my family; both my mother and husband have come before God. How fortunate we are! Later, I will preach to my daughter and friends, too. I will proclaim God's words and I want to say my heartfelt word: Behold! The scroll has been opened!"

Max

Max (2018) was born in the United States, but his parents soon returned with him to their home country, China. At age fourteen, he came back to the United States to attend high school. He was very concerned when he learned that his mother in China had converted to the CAG, as he searched for information on the Web and found various sites describing the movement as a "cult" guilty of serious crimes. He went to visit his mother and could not accept her claim that this time Jesus Christ had incarnated as a female. His mother repeated to Max the words of Almighty God: "Each stage of work done by God has a real significance. When Jesus arrived, He was male, and this time He is female. From this, you can see that God created both male and female for His work and with Him there is no distinction of gender." Gradually he was persuaded, particularly because he fellowshipped with members of the CAG and found them to be "normal" and pleasant people, not the violent "cultists" depicted on the anti-cult websites. But he was still disturbed by allegations of the church's crimes.

Finally, he overcame all his doubts after reading Almighty God's words. He learned:

> In the last days, under the guidance of God's words, more and more people are able to distinguish the evil forces that originate

from Satan. They also see clearly the satanic and demonic essence of the leaders of the [mainline] religious world and the atheistic political regime of the Chinese Communist Party.... Will Satan just do nothing as God comes to do the work of saving man and helping man break away from Satan's dark influence? It [the CAG always uses the impersonal "it" for Satan] is not willing to be defeated. In order to vie over God's chosen people with God, it will fight to the end. The religious world and the satanic CCP regime have teamed up together and through the internet and media, they spread rumors about and smear the name of the CAG without restraint in order to deceive those who do not have the truth or cannot distinguish. They are attempting to obtain control over the human race forever. (Max 2018)

But Max believes they will ultimately be defeated.

Tina and Charlie

Discovering the CAG through Facebook and being originally disturbed by the negative information on the internet are also part of the experience of Tina and Charlie, an American couple operating a small business in Arizona. I interviewed them after their conversion. Tina was a "seeker," curious about the future of humanity and the causes of the present troubles. She discovered the CAG on Facebook and started fellowshipping. Her daughter and husband were concerned that she spent too much time on her religious activities, and they also read that the CAG was a dangerous "cult." Tina, however, asked them whether, since she fellowshipped, she had become a better or worse mother and wife. They admitted she appeared to be calmer and more loving and caring.

Her daughter remained skeptical, but after Tina persuaded her husband, Charlie, to read *The Word Appears in the Flesh* he concluded that he "could not deny these words." An enthusiastic

Tina considered leaving her business and going to New York to work as a full-time missionary for the church. But, contrary to stereotypes depicting CAG as always insisting that converts become full-time missionaries, she was told that her duty was to remain with her family. She still encounters opposition based on charges that she has "joined a cult," but Tina and Charlie maintain a good relationship with their daughter and neighbors and do not despair of eventually bringing some of them to believe in Almighty God, not through insistence but through example, cordiality, and good grace.

Christopher

Christopher (2016; not his real name) was a pastor of the International Christian Life Center in the Philippines. Understandably his testimony is much more theological, yet it is grounded on his personal experience. He believed he was a good and effective Christian pastor, yet after years of service to his church he still looked on himself as a sinful and less than perfect human being, who easily lost his temper with his family. How was this possible, since he firmly believed he had been saved by Jesus? Almost by coincidence, when performing a different search on the internet, he found a CAG website, became interested in the church's theology, and wrote seeking a contact.

What won him over was the doctrine of the two stages of salvation and that "saved" and "purified" are different concepts. "I got to understand that being saved means that one has received Jesus' salvation, and will no longer be condemned . . . for violating the law. It doesn't mean that he has been completely purified." The sinful disposition remains, and is only being eradicated now, by the second appearance of Christ as Almighty God in the last days.

"I have believed in the Lord for so long," Christopher concluded,

> often gave sermons to believers, disciplined my body, yet I could not keep the Lord's way, living in sin and being unable to get rid

of it, and feeling agonized and distressed day after day. I finally understood at that time if people don't experience God's work of judgment and chastisement in the last days, they can never get rid of the bondage and shackles of sin on their own. Now I have beheld the path of achieving purification and reaching the true salvation. I am so grateful to God for His mercy and salvation upon me.... God's work is so practical. (Christopher 2016)

The Anti-Cult Perspective

Those opposed to "cults" dismiss the emic narratives of CAG members as deluded. For them, "cults" grow because they use sinister techniques of manipulation. They attribute the phenomenal growth of CAG to devious tactics, including brainwashing and even kidnapping members of other Christian churches to convert them. I will return to the latter accusation later in this book.

There is a large literature on conversion to religion in general and new religious movements in particular (for a survey, see Introvigne 2011). While anti-cultists have accused new religious movements of using sinister recruitment tools such as mind control and massive deception, scholars have found very little evidence of unusual missionary techniques, much less of their allegedly "magic" effectiveness (Barker 1984; Kilbourne and Richardson 1984, 1986; Robbins 1988; Richardson 1996; Lamb and Bryant 1999). Perhaps less exciting, scholars have concluded that, with rare exceptions, new religions convert new members and grow very much as the old ones do: by using preexisting family and friendship networks (Snow, Zurcher, and Ekland-Olson 1980, 1983). Most often people join a religion because families and friends introduce them to it (Stark and Roberts 1982).

Exceptions do exist, and it is occasionally argued that the CAG may be one, since its doctrine is accused of having a very low opinion of the family as an institution. A BBC 2014 report, which relied heavily on Chinese anti-cult sources, reported that, according to somebody who claimed to be a relative of a CAG member and whose attitude was obviously hostile, "The cult is anti-family.... It throw[s] away family relationships and encourage[s] each other to do the same.... Whoever is more resolute in rejecting their family is given a higher rank" (Gracie 2014).

In order to address this criticism, I will first examine whether the antifamily position of the CAG is confirmed by its doctrine and literature, and second, present the results of a survey conducted in 2018 among more than five hundred CAG members in South Korea, the U.S., and the Philippines (on which I first reported in Introvigne 2018d), most of them refugees from China, from which the traditional scholarly model predicting that religious conversion would normally happen *along*, rather than *against*, family networks appears to receive some additional support.

CAG Doctrine and the Family

As we know, the CAG believes that God's management for saving humankind is divided into three stages: the Age of Law (of Jehovah and the Old Testament), the Age of Grace (of Jesus Christ and the New Testament), and the Age of Kingdom (of Almighty God and *The Word Appears in the Flesh*). Since 1991 we have been living in the Age of Kingdom.

One basic truth remains through the different ages: God loves humanity. Since humankind is corrupted, God started what the CAG calls his "management plan," meaning his project for saving humankind. Since the time of the Flood and of Noah, God has been teaching people how to live a good, moral life on Earth and how to properly worship him. His teachings include specific requirements for the family, expressed in the Ten Commandments (which include "Honor your father and your mother," "You should not commit adultery," and "You should not covet your neighbor's wife") and reiterated by Jesus. The Ten Commandments are God's requirements and norms for humans in the Age of Law and remain valid in the Age of Grace and Age of Kingdom. With the passage to a new era, God has made higher practical requirements for humans, so that the Ten Commandments are somewhat less important in the Age of Kingdom, yet they are not entirely superseded. God's new requirement, based on the commands of the previous two ages, is that families shall allow themselves to be governed by God's words and truth and place themselves in the charge of Christ.

In the words of Almighty God:

> Today, what is required of you is not only limited to the Ten Commandments, but are commandments and laws that are higher than those of before, yet this does not mean that what came before has been abolished, for each stage of God's work is carried out upon the foundation of the stage that came before. That which Jehovah introduced to Israel, such as giving sacrifice, honoring your father and mother, not worshiping idols, not assaulting others, not cursing others, not committing adultery, not smoking, not drinking, not eating the dead, and not drinking blood, is it not the foundation for your practice even today? It is upon the foundation of the past that the work has been carried out up until today. Though the laws of the past are no longer mentioned, and new requirements have been made of you, these laws have not been abolished, and instead, they have been uplifted. To say that they have been abolished means that the previous age is outdated, yet there are some commandments that you must always honor. (The Church of Almighty God 2017e, 790)

Among the latter, there are God's requirements concerning the family. Almighty God teaches that the family exists because of God's sovereignty and arrangement, and is a positive feature of human society. "Were it not for the Creator's predestination and His guidance, a life newly born into this world would not know where to go or where to stay, would have no relations, belong nowhere, have no real home. But because of the Creator's meticulous arrangements, it begins the journey of its life with a place to stay, parents, a place it belongs to, and relatives" (The Church of Almighty God 2017e, 1822). Here Almighty God explains that the course of human life—birth, growing up, independence, marriage, progeny, death—is fully dominated and preordained by the Creator.

In the words of Zhao Weishan, CAG's administrative leader, "Getting married and having children originate from God's creation and predestination. It was God who initially created man and woman in order for mankind to reproduce and multiply. This is an indisputable fact. Since getting married and having children originate from God, therefore they are positive things. This is undeniable" (The Church of Almighty God 2017b, 114).

Some members of the CAG leave their home and devote their lives to a full-time missionary career. Some criticize this decision as "breaking family ties," but it is hardly unique to the CAG (see Matthew 10:38; Luke 14:26; 18:29–30; 9:62). Jesus himself expressed this ideal: "If any man come to me, and hate not his father, and mother, and wife, and children, and brothers, and sisters, yes, and his own life also, he cannot be my disciple. And whoever does not bear his cross, and come after me, cannot be my disciple. . . . So likewise, whoever he be of you that forsakes not all that he has, he cannot be my disciple" (Luke 14:26–27, 33).

While some critics claim that CAG leaders interfere with the choices of devotees about their marriages and that whoever refuses marriage is given a higher rank in the church, this is contrary to the teachings of Almighty God, who insists:

> When God acts, He does not coerce people. For example, whether you get married should be according to your own actual situation; the truth has been clearly spoken to you, and I do not restrain you. Some families oppress people to the extent that they're unable to believe in God unless they get married—so marriage, conversely, is to their advantage. For some people, marriage not only

brings no benefits, but costs them what they originally had. This must depend on your actual circumstances and your own resolution. I do not come up with rules by which to make demands of you. (The Church of Almighty God 2017e, 982)

Almighty God explains, "During the previous age, what was the principle behind when people were used? Whoever could sing and dance, or was oldest and unmarried, had pride of place. . . . We don't care about that. We look at man's substance, because the key to believing in God is what a person's substance is like, and whether they are able to worship God" (The Church of Almighty God 2018a).

Church teachings harshly denounce sexual immorality in terms that are not dissimilar from traditional Protestant Evangelical preaching on sexual sins. Almighty God admonishes:

> Sexually immoral, lascivious men always want to pull those coquettish harlots to them for their own enjoyment. I will not save such sexually immoral demons, I hate you filthy demons, your lasciviousness and coquettishness have plunged you into hell—what have you to say for yourselves? You filthy demons and evil spirits are so heinous! You're disgusting! How could such trash be saved? Could those ensnared in sin still be saved? These truths, this way, and this life hold no attraction to you; you're attracted to sinfulness, to money, standing, fame and gain, the enjoyments of the flesh, the handsomeness of men and coquettishness of women. What qualifies you to enter My kingdom? (The Church of Almighty God 2017e, 988)

Zhao also urges CAG believers to respect and honor marriage: "If the person has a husband (or wife), then you need to respect this person's marriage. You cannot interfere with someone's marriage; to respect others is to respect yourself, if you do not respect others then you do not respect yourself. If you respect others, then others will respect you. If in your heart you do not respect marriage, then you do not have humanity. If you are able to respect marriage, if you are able to love others and respect others, then you will not do things that harm others" (The Church of Almighty God 2018a).

CAG websites often publish testimonies of devotees who claim that their family life has been made more harmonious by conversion to Almighty God and that old problems have been solved (see, e.g., Xiaolin 2016; Haohao 2017; Panpan 2017; Xia 2017; Zhien 2017), although in some cases divorce and remarriage occurred. The CAG does not exclude divorce: members may receive advice from the church leaders but ultimately take their own decisions according to their situation.

As happens in all missionary religions, members are counseled to share their faith with their families. However, one of the "Ten Administrative Decrees That Must Be Obeyed by God's Chosen People in the Age of Kingdom," proclaimed by Almighty God, states, "Kin who are not of the faith (your children, your husband or wife, your sisters or your parents, and so on) should not be forced into the church. God's household is not short of members, and there is no need to make up its numbers with people who have no use. All those who do not believe gladly must not be led into the church. This decree is directed at all people" (The Church of Almighty God 2017e, 1458).

There are family members who may be hostile to their CAG relatives, or who do not share the choice of some members to devote their lives to a full-time missionary career. Some members report they have been encouraged by their local community to become missionaries, although the final decision is always left to the individual. But these problems occur in all religions and are hardly unique to the CAG. Zhao insists that nobody should be forced to serve as a full-time missionary: "Dedicating one's entire being to expend for God should be based on one's own choice. Some people dedicate themselves to spread the gospel, others serve in churches. Some people dedicate their entire being to expend for God full time. Others can only expend themselves for God part of the time. This all depends on the choices people are willing to make; God's family does not force people to do things" (The Church of Almighty God 2017b, 36).

Obviously, it is a different situation when families are separated because CAG members are arrested or forced to flee China. CCP media claim that the CAG separates families, yet CAG's literature notes that it is the same CCP that in many cases is responsible for the separation of Christian families. In one of the movies produced by the CAG in South Korea, *Red Re-Education at Home*, a devotee forcefully makes this point with his mother. "Many Christians," he states, "were displaced and rendered homeless. So many people were arrested and imprisoned, and some were even persecuted to death! The CCP government is the culprit behind the ruination of countless Christian families. But it counterclaimed that the families of these people were ruined by their belief in God. Isn't this a distortion of the facts and turning black-and-white on its head? Had it not been for the CCP's lunatic suppression, arrest and torture of Christians, would it have led to such an outcome? Isn't this the sin committed by the CCP through its persecution of Christians?" (Chen, Yin, and Wu 2017).

Several movies produced by CAG promote family values, and some of them focus on the crisis of contemporary families and problems such as the consequences of divorce (*Where Is My Home*, Huang, Zhang, and Zhang 2017) and teenage internet addiction (*Child, Come Back Home*, Zheng and Li 2017). The orientation of these movies toward traditional Christian family values is easily recognizable and explains why they are appreciated by many who do not share CAG's theological perspectives (Introvigne 2017b).

That CAG's theology is antifamily does not seem to find any support in the church's scriptures, which teach that the family exists because of God's sovereignty and orchestration, and reiterate that God's requirements of honoring parents and respecting marriage are still very much in force in the Age of Kingdom.

Survey Results

In 2017, I conducted interviews of CAG members in several countries (Europe, U.S., and South Korea; other countries followed in 2018 and 2019). Most were Chinese refugees, and most reported they had been converted (had "returned to Almighty God," in CAG's language) through relatives. I also interviewed some American (non-Chinese) converts who had started interacting with CAG members on Facebook, then met them in person and joined the church.

I decided to conduct a more systematic survey by administering questionnaires to CAG members in countries other than Mainland China, where, because of the persecution, any survey would be impossible. I used a computer-assisted anonymized survey from one of the simplest programs, Google Forms, considering that some of the refugees who had just escaped China might be less comfortable using more sophisticated tools. Four Google Forms addresses were set up, respectively, for the large Chinese-speaking congregation in Seoul, for the Korean-speaking congregation in Seoul, for the congregations in the United States, and for the congregations in the Philippines. The websites allowed respondents to answer in English, Chinese, Korean, Spanish, and Tagalog (Filipino). Flyers with invitations in these languages to participate voluntarily and anonymously in a sociological survey were distributed at the largest CAG fellowship meetings in the following locations: Seoul (Chinese-language fellowship); Seoul (Korean-language fellowship); Flushing, New York; Lebanon, Virginia; Grand Marais, Michigan; Golden Valley, Arizona; Los Angeles, California; Manila, Philippines; Cebu, Philippines; Davao, Philippines; Iloilo, Philippines.

Flyers were distributed in South Korea on January 21, 2018; in the Philippines on January 24, 27, and 28, 2018; and in the United States on January 27, February 3, and February 4, 2018. The flyers requested that the survey be completed by February 28, 2018. In South Korea and in the United States (except in Grand Marais and Golden Valley), I distributed the flyers personally, and I was allowed to explain the aims of the survey. In Golden Valley, Grand Marais, and the Philippines, local church members distributed the flyers. Since the Chinese-speaking members in Korea, the Korean-speaking members there, the members in the United States, and the members in the Philippines used four different websites for answering the survey, I was able to determine how many answered and submitted complete and usable forms for each subgroup: 66 in the United States, 34 in the Korean-speaking congregation and 347 in the Chinese-speaking congregation in Seoul; 69 in the Philippines. With respect to the number of distributed questionnaires, the ratio of respondents was 57.5% among Chinese-speaking congregations and 69% among Korean-speaking congregations in Seoul, 68% in the Philippines, and 69.3% in the United States.

The questionnaires asked respondents to identify themselves as:

- A Chinese who returned to Almighty God in China.
- A Chinese who returned to Almighty God abroad.
- A non-Chinese who returned to Almighty God abroad.

The answers confirmed that CAG communities overseas currently include a majority of refugees from China: 337 of my 516 respondents (65.31%) "returned to Almighty God" in China, and only 10 were Chinese who converted abroad (1.94%). However, the percentage of non-Chinese new converts, 169, or roughly one-third of the sample (32.75%), was not insignificant. They included 34 Koreans, 66 Americans, and 69 Filipinos. It is probably too early to refer to the CAG as a global rather than a Chinese movement. At the same time, earlier studies ignoring non-Chinese converts are becoming rapidly outdated. It is also worth noting that, in 2016, Spain became the first country to legally recognize the CAG as a religion. It was registered in the Ministry of Justice's Register of Religious Entities on October 10, 2016 (Ministerio de Justicia 2016). Other new religious movements have struggled for years to be registered there.

Before converting, respondents should have heard positive information about the CAG, as distinguished from plentiful hostile news and reports that abound in Chinese official media. The survey asked them for the source of this positive information. Possible answers included:

- Brochure or book.
- Internet.
- Member of my family.
- Friend.
- Missionary of the CAG.
- Other.

Table 4.1 presents the answers to this question.

Keeping in mind that the question is not about conversion but about the sources where respondents first encountered positive information about the CAG, a significant difference between Chinese who converted in China and non-Chinese who converted abroad emerges. The third group, Chinese who converted abroad, is small, but missionaries were as important for them as family members. For those Chinese who converted in China, however, where CAG

Table 4.1 Sources of First (Positive) Information about the CAG

Groups	Converted in China	Chinese, Converted Abroad	Non-Chinese	Total
Literature	5	0	0	5
Internet	0	0	68	68
Family member	255	4	17	276
Friend	52	1	72	125
Missionary	24	4	11	39
Other	1	1	1	3
Total	337	10	169	516

websites and most international social networks are blocked by the authorities, it was overwhelmingly family members who first supplied the future convert with positive information about the CAG: 255 out of 337, or 75.67%. Friends came second (52), at a distant 15.43%, and CAG missionaries (24) were the first source of positive information in only 7.12% of the cases. The internet (68), on the other hand, was a significant source for those 169 non-Chinese who converted abroad (40.24%), even if friends (72) were more important (42.60%) than family members (17, 10.06%) or missionaries (11, 6.51%), although it is possible that in some cases respondents met missionaries on the internet.

It is also interesting to note, as detailed in Table 4.2, the prevailing role of the internet among non-Chinese converts in the U.S., while in South Korea and the Philippines networks of friends appeared to be more important. From previous in-person interviews I learned that these networks often consisted of members of the congregations of other Christian churches, who converted en masse to the CAG, in at least one Filipino case following their pastor.

Question 2 of the survey asked, "Who was the most influential person (apart from Almighty God) helping you in returning to Almighty God?" Possible answers included:

Table 4.2 Sources of First (Positive) Information about the CAG among Non-Chinese Converts

Non-Chinese Converts	South Korea	USA	Philippines	Total
Literature	0	0	0	0
Internet	1	54	13	68
Family member	7	7	3	17
Friend	20	0	52	72
Missionary	6	5	0	11
Other	0	0	1	1
Total	34	66	69	169

- A member of my immediate family (parent, brother or sister, son or daughter) who already believed in Almighty God.
- Another relative who already believed in Almighty God.
- A CAG missionary I met personally.
- A CAG missionary I met via the internet.
- A friend who already believed in Almighty God.
- Other.

As shown in Table 4.3, the sample of Chinese who converted abroad is too small to support conclusions, although the internet seems to have played a significant role in these conversions. Again we find a difference between Chinese and non-Chinese members. In China, a solid majority (212, 62.91%) was converted by members of their immediate family, and another 7.12% (24) by more distant relatives. Missionaries, although operating under the threat of persecution, did play a role (63, 18.69%), as did friends (31, 9.20%), but most members were converted by their families. In contrast to these results, family members (8, 4.73%) and relatives (3, 1.77%) were not very significant for the conversion of non-Chinese members abroad, where the internet (89, 52.66%) accounted for the majority of conversions. Table 4.4 shows the greater influence of the internet

Table 4.3 Agents of Conversion

Groups	Converted in China	Chinese, Converted Abroad	Non-Chinese	Total
Family	212	1	8	221
Relative	24	1	3	28
Missionary	63	2	16	81
Internet	0	6	89	95
Friend	31	0	52	83
Other	7	0	1	8
Total	337	10	169	516

Table 4.4 Agents of Conversion for Foreign Converts

Non-Chinese Converts	South Korea	USA	Philippines	Total
Family	5	1	2	8
Relative	2	0	1	3
Missionary	11	5	0	16
Internet	16	60	13	89
Friend	0	0	52	52
Other	0	0	1	1
Total	34	66	69	169

in the U.S. and that of friends in the Philippines, probably for the reason I mentioned earlier.

It is possible, as suggested in some of my interviews, that conversion through the family in China is overrepresented among CAG members who escaped overseas, the only ones who were able to participate in the survey. The case of whole congregations who converted to the CAG led by their pastors is not unique to the Philippines but also happened in China. These large communities of CAG believers are somewhat less likely to flee abroad en masse than are individual members. Certainly I do not argue that the CAG relies *only* on family networks for its growth, although data show they play a significant role.

These comments on foreign converts are supported by in-person interviews I did before the survey. Typical of these foreign converts were Tina and Charlie, the American couple from Arizona. Recall that the wife started interacting with CAG members on Facebook, then met them in person, converted, and persuaded her husband to join the church. After reading passages of Almighty God's words in *The Word Appears in the Flesh*, Charlie concluded that those words "were all from God." He explained his reasoning: "It's very touching. It's deep words that, you know, only God could speak to you through. It's very powerful to know that of this time, he is speaking to my heart through his words. And nobody's able to do that." His wife tried unsuccessfully to do the same with her adult daughter, but the daughter was influenced by negative information on the CAG she had found on the internet and did not respond positively.

It should be reiterated that the etic study of how conversions happen should remain in dialogue with the emic perception of conversions by believers. They insist that, although there are different ways of spreading the Gospel, whether or not one converts is entirely voluntary and ultimately depends on one's readiness to listen to the voice of Almighty God and recognize Almighty God as the returned Jesus Christ, the only true God.

Once converted, CAG members, as is typical of most converts, tried to convert others to their newly discovered faith. Question 3 asked, "Did you ever try to help members of your family return to Almighty God?" The CAG is an intensely missionary religion, and only a small portion of the respondents (67, 12.98%, vs. 430, 83.33%) indicated that, after joining, they did not try to convert their families (see Table 4.5). Not all these conversion attempts were successful, either in China or overseas. Chinese family members may have been afraid of being subject to the CCP's persecution or influenced by propaganda against the church. The problems of my Arizona couple with their daughter indicate that converting family members can also be difficult in the U.S. because families of converts find a good deal of negative information about the CAG on the internet (see Heggie 2017).

Table 4.5 CAG Devotees Who Tried to Convert Family Members

Converted Family Members	Converted in China	Chinese, Converted Abroad	South Koreans	American	Filipino	Total
Yes	278	6	33	44	69	430
No	40	4	1	22	0	67
Other	19	0	0	0	0	19
Total	337	10	34	66	69	516

Conclusion

Both the analysis of CAG's literature and the utterances of Almighty God, which are normative for the church, and the survey demonstrated that the CAG is not against the family. Conversion to the CAG is not dissimilar from conversion to many other new religious movements. According to the survey, the overwhelming majority of those who converted in China (70.03%) did so because of a family member or relative, although other forms of conversion may be underrepresented among CAG members who escaped overseas and participated in the survey. In turn, 82.49% of those who converted in China and 83.33% of the total sample tried to convert their family members. As is common in other religions, conversion often took place along family networks, and rumors that the CAG grew through unusual or sinister tactics appear to be just another instance of stereotypes targeting "cults."

There is, however, an area where the CAG appears to grow through novel strategies, including a liberal use of the internet: the West. Outside China, and particularly in the United States, the CAG is too new and too small to make use of preexisting family networks. Most of its members are refugees from China with little or no connections in their host country. However, the CAG manages to grow by approaching potential converts on social networks such as Facebook. There are also CAG apps for smartphones and pop-up chats on several CAG websites.

The strategy of privileging the internet has so far elicited good results in the U.S. It is too early to say whether the church will continue to use this strategy or, as the church grows outside of Mainland China, more traditional methods of conversion will become more important than the internet, when local communities will be consolidated in new countries.

5
Living in The Church of Almighty God

Organization and Demographics

Because the CAG is banned in China, its members, including refugees abroad, are understandably reluctant to discuss its organizational details. This occasionally gives outside observers the impression that the CAG is just a loose network of believers, without the kind of organization that would justify its definition as a religion. However, this impression is inaccurate (Dunn 2015; Introvigne 2018b).

The CAG insists on strict adherence to its normative scripture, *The Word Appears in the Flesh*, which includes "Ten Administrative Decrees That Must Be Obeyed by God's Chosen People in the Age of Kingdom" and "Seventeen Commandments That Must Be Obeyed by God's Chosen People in the Age of Kingdom," which are similar in style to the Ten Commandments of the Bible. Those who disobey these decrees and commandments, either doctrinally or morally, and do not repent, are expelled. In fact, this is a frequent occurrence in the CAG, with some sources reporting 300,000 to 500,000 expulsions (CESNUR 2017). As happens in all successful religious movements, dissent and schisms have also occurred, with some members overtly challenging the Man Used by the Holy Spirit or the arrangements of the church's work he issued, and even identifying themselves as a new Almighty God. These members were expelled as "Antichrists" or "False Christs," together with those of their followers who showed no remorse after an attempt at correction (see Pan 2015; Ling 2015; both articles rely heavily on hostile sources). According to my interviews on this subject with leaders and members in South Korea and the U.S. in January 2019, the agreement of 80% of the members of the local community, followed by a determination by the leadership, is needed to ratify an expulsion.

When interviewed about their leaders, refugees often answer that in the CAG there are no leaders. This may give the mistaken impression that the CAG is loosely organized, while it is in fact highly structured. There is a theological reason for the refugees' answer: they are referring to the Gospel of Matthew (23:8–10), where Jesus taught his followers to "call no man master," which refugees interpret as "call no human being leader."

Another problem is that refugees who are interviewed by immigration officers tell their stories in Chinese, and most interpreters would translate the English word "leader" as *ling dao ren* (领导人). The word phonetically resembles the English "leader" but in Chinese denotes an authoritarian leadership. CAG members would have no quarrel with the word *dai ling* (带领), which is another possible translation of "leader," and would admit they have "leaders" if this translation was used. In fact, there is no doubt that the CAG has leaders in the common sense of the word.

The highest administrative leader of the Church is Zhao Weishan, whose interpretation of the words of Almighty God is accepted as authoritative by CAG members. There are also different levels of elected local leaders, called in China church leaders (*dai ling*), subdistrict leaders, and district leaders, appointed on the basis of the number of CAG members in the corresponding areas. A church leader normally oversees a community of at least twenty but fewer than fifty members. If the group grows to exceed fifty, a separate community is established under a new church leader. There are also national leaders in the diaspora countries, although in some countries they do not appear at public events and use their religious rather than their civil names, for fear that their position will cause retaliation against their relatives in China.

The CAG has developed an effective, if clandestine, system of contacting leaders of the different communities in China from abroad. This allows the communities in the diaspora to rapidly obtain confirmation that those arriving from China are really members of the CAG and not spies sent by the Chinese government nor economic immigrants falsely claiming membership in the church for the purpose of obtaining asylum. When new refugees belonged to a local community in China from which some have already expatriated, their brother or sister church members can vouch for them.

In her 2015 book, Dunn reported that, according to previous studies, CAG and other new religious movements in China were "primarily attracting middle-aged and elderly women of relatively low educational attainment" (58). For some reason, journalistic sources have often incorrectly quoted Dunn as describing CAG as composed *only* by barely literate peasants. More problematic is the fact that hundreds of interviews by scholars, including this author, conducted in 2017, 2018, and 2019 among the diaspora communities, found that most members (although not all, and with differences between one country and the other) were young and middle class and had a good education. There were indeed more women than men. Some had received appropriate artistic training in China, which obviously is not typically the case for middle-aged peasants, and the flourishing of the arts in the diaspora was made possible with their help.

A Minimalist but Rich Worship

The core of the life of the CAG is the relationship of each believer with Almighty God. As Folk (2018, 62) found, for church members God is both "near and far." Almighty God is referred to as "the Practical God," for in the Age of Kingdom, God is not an idea or a theory but a living person with a divine substance. At the same time, few members have ever met the person they worship as Almighty God, and most do not know the civil name of the person the CAG recognizes as Almighty God. They refuse to acknowledge surnames such as Yang or Deng attributed to Almighty God by outsiders, and claim they never heard them mentioned within the CAG.

As mentioned earlier, members believe Almighty God incarnated as a woman but refer to her as "he" to emphasize the fact that it is the same God who manifested as Jehovah in the time of the Old Testament and Jesus in the New Testament. Folk (2018, 62) observes that "the CAG's brothers and sisters think that it is more important to know the truth and God's substance through experiencing his [Almighty God's] words than knowing the details of God's incarnated life. They claim that in the Age of Grace the early Christians had a similar attitude with respect to Jesus Christ."

There is no formal liturgy in the CAG, nor sacraments such as baptism or eucharist, nor are Christmas or Easter celebrated. The CAG believes that its members "must worship [God] in spirit and in truth" (John 4:24) in their meetings and that traditional Christian sacraments were practices of the Age of Grace, which have no place in the Age of Kingdom, just as the practices of the Age of Law, including the Sabbath, were no longer required for Christians in the Age of Grace.

However, this does not mean that gathering together is not important for members. They fellowship regularly by studying and discussing Almighty God's words, hearing sermons, singing hymns, and sharing testimonies. CAG members take turns reading the words of Almighty God and sharing their understanding. The intensity of the religious life contrasts with a minimalist style of worship.

Fellowshipping for those outside Mainland China today is often done on the internet, and it may happen that believers from different countries and even different continents fellowship together. Members describe this as an exciting experience. They note that they have frequent occasions to speak and express their views, contrasting this with the "passive" attitude toward the pastor's or priest's sermons in the mainline churches.

After visiting communities of the CAG in the U.S., Canada, South Korea, Italy, France, Finland, Greece, Switzerland, Spain, Japan, Taiwan, Belgium, Hungary, the Netherlands, and Australia, I find that many observers have overlooked one aspect of life and worship in the CAG. For many CAG brothers and sisters, cultivating beauty through the arts is a form of worship. Without understanding their approach to beauty and the visual arts, an essential part of the CAG experience is missing.

A Theology of Beauty

An important, if often overlooked, belief of the CAG is its doctrine of beauty. One of the consequences of the persecution was that the church was limited in how it could promote and organize artistic activities and did not produce a systematic doctrine of aesthetics nor specific teachings about the arts. The flourishing of the arts after 2014 among the communities that could freely practice their religion outside China was premised on the holy scripture of the CAG, *The Word Appears in the Flesh*, which includes a theory of beauty.

Beauty is, first, an inherent feature of the words of Almighty God, described as uniformly "beautiful and moving" (The Church of Almighty God 2017e, 3). The presence of Almighty God on Earth is not only momentous and decisive; it also creates unprecedented beauty (34). One of the distinctive characters of the new kingdom of God is beauty (46, 88). *The Word Appears in the Flesh* also mentions the "piteous state" of those who, remaining outside the new kingdom, are deprived of this beauty, "watching the beautiful scenes within the kingdom but unable to enter" (166).

Believers respond to this divine beauty by producing beauty on Earth. This beauty manifests first in the life itself of the believers. The testimony and the strenuous activities of the followers of Almighty God are in themselves "beautiful" (The Church of Almighty God 2017e, 9). Beauty, however, is also produced in an artistic form. The utterances mention the "most beautiful songs" (34), but visual arts would soon follow in the experience of the believing community.

Visual Arts in the Diaspora

Understandably, controversies and persecution in China have dominated the scholarly study of the CAG, and the church's artistic production has been almost totally neglected. However, after 2014, when a significant number of church members managed to flee China, they were able to practice their religion freely and openly. An important artistic production followed. Between 2014 and 2018 CAG members produced some 2,400 paintings and 80 movies, as well as more than 730 religious videos, including videos of Almighty God's words, of hymns, and of personal experiences. Most of the movies and videos were distributed and released online for free in a variety of languages.

If we distinguish art produced by religious movements as *internal*, created mostly for the purposes of beautifying the places of worship and illustrate missionary material, and *external*, influenced by religious teachings but largely destined for art galleries and the market (Introvigne 2017d), we should place the production of the CAG in the category of internal art. However, some of the movies entered what I have called the "semi-external" field (Introvigne 2017d). They were originally produced for missionary and educational purposes, but their quality was appreciated by critics and audiences on the Christian film festival circuit, particularly in United States. Although the theology underlying these film festivals was very far from that of the CAG, the festivals nonetheless honored some of the movies, including the musical *Xiaozhen's Story*, the docudrama *Chronicles of Religious Persecution in China*

(Introvigne 2017b), and the musical documentary *The One Who Holds Sovereignty over Everything* with several awards.

This did not happen with the paintings, however, because the way they came to the attention of a larger audience was by being featured in the movies and videos. The artists normally prefer not to sign their works. Some decorate the places of worship and buildings of the CAG in Korea and elsewhere, and reproductions appear in the private homes of the believers. A small exhibition was organized in South Korea, and larger exhibitions are a possibility for the future, considering that the technical quality of some of the paintings is above average. The style is conventional and rooted in traditional Christian illustrations of the Bible, while the scenes from Chinese history and mythology are influenced by both Chinese classical paintings and the contemporary Oriental comics known as manga.

The quality is achieved in most (but not all) cases by a generous use of computer-assisted painting. David Hockney and other luminaries of contemporary art insist that the use of computers does not take the works outside the realm of art, provided that human creativity still prevails on the suggestions offered by the software (Miller 2014). Nor are all the church's actors and painters amateurs; as mentioned earlier, some had a professional education before leaving China, and most of them continued to be educated in the arts in South Korea and elsewhere, although none makes art his or her main profession.

South Korea is the prevailing center of artistic production; most of the movies were produced there, although Spain has also a sizable contingent of members of the church skilled in singing and dancing. Movies are normally shot indoor, with a liberal use of electronic effects. As for the paintings, there are two series of importance, one biblical and one about China. The biblical images often emphasize messages typical of the CAG.

One example is a painting of Adam and Eve after they committed the original sin. Although the style is somewhat cartoonish, what is important here is that the center of the image is not occupied by the two progenitors but by the clothes with which they will be able to cover themselves, overcoming their newly discovered shame of being naked. The clothes, skin robes with one shoulder strap, are the center because, according to the Book of Genesis (3:21), God made them with his own hands. Although humans sin, God loves them to the point of taking personal care of their clothing. What is really at the center of the painting thus is God's love.

Another Old Testament example is a painting depicting the joy of Noah's family after the Flood has ended. While most classic renderings of the same scene place at the center either Noah or the ark, here the attention of the viewer is immediately captured by the rainbow, which symbolizes God's promise that he will not again destroy his people with a flood. The church teaches that even today rainbows appear to remind us of God's love. Again the real center of the painting is the love of God.

God, however, can be angry or sad as well as happy. In another painting we see Jesus scolding the Pharisees, where the Lord's expression is far from conventional sweetness. Believers will certainly interpret the painting as a reminder not to be present-day Pharisees, rejecting God and incurring his condemnation.

Two beloved images, ubiquitous wherever members gather, represent, respectively, Jesus knocking at the door and the crucifixion of Peter. The first composition exhibits Pre-Raphaelite reminiscences, and the well-known *The Light of the World* by William Holman Hunt comes to mind when the rhythm of the image is considered. The second places Peter in a landscape featuring pine trees and rocks, which symbolize the determination and the solidity of Peter's testimony.

As mentioned earlier, movies and videos produced by the CAG, including *The Mystery of Godliness—The Sequel* (2017), won awards at international film festivals. *The Mystery of Godliness* tells the story of an old Chinese preacher, Lin Bo-en, who converts to the CAG and is persecuted and discriminated against by both the regime and the mainline Christian churches. The movie presents lively debates about the incarnation of God, connected with the title's theme, which refers to the film's message, which expounds the CAG's theology about the new incarnation of God comprehensively and systematically. In the musical documentary *The One Who Holds Sovereignty over Everything* (2018), a theological view of human history is presented through a series of distinguished performances of the CAG choir.

The award-winning movie *Chronicles of Religious Persecution in China* (2017) is centered on the tragedy of a church member who was tortured to death while in custody, although his death was officially declared a suicide. It is certainly a movie with an agenda, but the rhythm is engaging.

The church earned additional awards with its musical movies (Introvigne 2017b). Together with theological content, they feature well-choreographed dances and songs, with both traditional Chinese and contemporary elements. *Every Nation Worships the Practical God* (an expression, as we have seen, typical of the church to indicate the present-day Almighty God) portrays the reactions of different groups of people confronted with the unexpected news that God has returned to Earth. The song lyrics are taken from the very utterances of Almighty God. *Human Beings Have Regained the Sanctity They Once Possessed* (2016) converts into a musical the apocalyptic theme of the confrontation between God and Satan in the last days. Just when Satan, the great red dragon, seems to prevail and the world is on the verge of annihilation, the lightning flashes forth from the East: Almighty God, the Christ of the last days, comes to Earth personally and speaks words that are used as weapons by God's people to defeat Satan. In God's majestic judgment, Satan is revealed in its true form and eventually reduced to ashes by Almighty God's wrath. Then Almighty God will bring his people into the new Heaven and new Earth, where all will enjoy a beautiful life.

Xiaozhen's Story is one of the most successful musical movies produced by the CAG to date and has won an impressive number of awards at different Christian film festivals. Released in November 2015, it is a morality tale, the story of a girl who feels betrayed by her friends and sinks into a false life of materialism and sin, where all the characters wear animal masks. By accepting Almighty God, Xiaozhen is able to remove her mask and get back in touch with her deeper self and with God. The story may appear moralistic, but the quality performance of the girl playing the title role, the wise use of the electronic stage, and the peculiar beauty of the songs rescue an otherwise conventional plot and justify the awards.

6
Fake News
The McDonald's Murder of 2014

Academic Studies of Fake News

A growing academic literature has examined the concept of fake news (see Introvigne 2018c), false information deliberately circulated and presented in such a way that many will believe it is true. Contemporary fake news goes beyond traditional disinformation, with an unprecedented ability to mislead the public by using a variety of media to create images that appear authoritative and believable. Classical Cold War disinformation by both the Soviets and the Americans had similar aims but lacked the resources of contemporary technology and social media. Building on the terminology adopted by the philosophers Neil Levy (2017, 20) and Regina Rini (2017, E45), another philosopher, the University of Berlin's Axel Gelfert (2018, 108), proposed the following definition: "Fake news is the deliberate presentation of (typically) false or misleading claims *as news*, where the claims are misleading *by design*." Gelfert argues that skilled producers of fake news exploit four preexisting cognitive biases: the confirmation bias (we normally accept new information if it confirms our beliefs and prejudices); the repetition effect ("if they keep repeating it, it should be true"); priming (use of words that trigger a nonconscious memory reaction, such as "cult"); and affective arousal (emotions lower our defenses against fake news, for example when we hear that "they abuse children" or "kill people"; 111–13).

Well before the expression "fake news" became fashionable, scholars of religion noticed how rumors were spread against "bad" religions and made credible by both their reiteration and their endorsement by supposedly authoritative sources. As early as 1960, David Brion Davis studied how what we would today call fake news was spread in the nineteenth century against Catholicism and other minority religions in the United States. The same phenomenon was noticed with respect to "cults" during the "cult wars" (Richardson 1978, 1979, 1993; Gallagher 2016).

In all these cases, however, the fake news about religions labeled "heresies" or "cults" was spread by private entrepreneurs: secular antireligious activists or anti-cultists, or rival religionists. In recent years we have witnessed the spread of fake news about religious movements organized, in a much more systematic way, not by private but by public actors. In 2017, for example, the Jehovah's Witnesses were "liquidated" and banned in Russia. The Putin administration was obviously annoyed by the almost unanimous condemnation of this move by international organizations, Western states, academics, and leading NGOs in Russia and abroad (Introvigne 2018h). One of the results of this situation was a flourishing of blogs, groups, and social network pages accusing the Jehovah's Witnesses of a great variety of wrongdoings, most of them ostensibly managed by people presenting themselves as former Witnesses. No doubt, several of these websites were genuine expressions of the anger of disgruntled former members. However, their simultaneous appearances in different countries in the weeks after the Russian liquidation decision may not have been entirely coincidental.

China has deployed a similarly massive action to justify its persecution of movements on its lists of *xie jiao*. In recent years, Chinese propaganda supporting the anti-xie-jiao campaigns has focused on the CAG. In June 2017, for example, the CAG leaked to a number of scholars (including the present author) a document allegedly transcribing the content of a teleconference of June 16, 2014, wherein officers of the Chinese Central Office for the Prevention and Handling of Cults (also referred to as Central Office 610) discussed the CAG. They recommended, "Firmly grasp the typical case of 'May 28 McDonald's Murder' in one hand to expose the reactionary nature, deceptive tricks and serious threats of the cult... [and] vigorously promote foreign projects [of propaganda]." As we will see in this chapter, the "May 28 McDonald's Murder" was a crime committed in 2014 by a religious group different from the CAG and transformed by Chinese propaganda into a CAG crime through a massive operation of fake news spread both at home and internationally.

For whatever reason, these operations found a particularly receptive audience in British media, including the most prestigious ones. After the 2014 McDonald's case, both the BBC (Gracie 2014) and *The Telegraph* (Moore 2015) reported on the CAG through their correspondents in Beijing, who used documents supplied by the Chinese authorities and already published by Chinese official media. These reports were particularly uncritical and blindly followed Chinese propaganda; unfortunately they were quoted in the following years by immigration authorities and courts denying refugee status to members of the CAG who had escaped abroad. *The Telegraph*'s correspondent was perhaps the only Western journalist who accepted at face value a twenty-two-page document circulated by the Chinese authorities, accusing CAG authorities in New York of instructing their followers in China to kill CCP members, explaining, "If they murder Communist party members, 'the spirit of the Great Red Dragon will no longer possess them'" (Moore 2015). The language, the theology, and the style of the document are not typical of the CAG, and even Chinese government media have not accused members of the CAG of any such murder. By doing some homework, even a nonspecialized journalist should have recognized the document as a vulgar forgery fabricated by Chinese propaganda agents. Yet in 2017, I counted some twenty thousand media pages in different languages connecting the CAG, or Eastern Lightning, with the McDonald's murder. Obviously this particular fake news campaign has been fairly successful (Introvigne 2017c).

Enter the Scholars

One of the reasons Chinese propaganda about the CAG went unchallenged for many years was that few, if any, scholars had paid any attention to the church. An Australian PhD student, Emily Dunn, published two short pioneer articles in 2008, followed by her dissertation in 2010, which was the basis for a book published in 2015. Meanwhile, in 2011, a master's thesis on the CAG was produced by a student at Shandong University, but it was largely a compilation of police and anti-cult sources (Fang 2011). Dunn's role as the first non-Chinese scholar who studied the CAG should be acknowledged. However, she admitted that she relied only on internet sources (some primary and posted by the CAG, others from obviously biased Chinese media) and on her interviews in China of Chinese police officers and others hostile to the CAG. She did not interview a single member of the CAG, and in fact reported that she went to New York looking for the local community but had the wrong address and was not able to find it (Dunn 2015, 23); this happened in 2013, while today in New York, South Korea, Spain and elsewhere the communities of the CAG have very visible religious buildings that are more difficult to miss. Interestingly, several English-speaking CAG members I interviewed had read Dunn's 2015 book and some of her articles and vocally expressed their disagreement with her presentation of the church.

In the meantime, American and European scholars of new religious movements, some of them veterans of the "cult wars" and familiar with the dynamics of anti-cult propaganda, started studying the CAG from a different angle and lecturing on their findings at international conferences. In 2017 five Western scholars who had become familiar with the CAG, including Gordon Melton, Holly Folk, and I, were invited to two conferences, in Zhengzhou and Hong Kong, on (or, rather, *against*) the CAG, by the Chinese Anti-Xie-Jiao Association, which has direct ties with the CCP. Chinese government-controlled media claimed that the Western scholars were finally persuaded that the position of the Chinese authorities was justified (see, e.g., *KKNews* 2017), but in fact we went to China with the goal of challenging the government's view of "cults."

The Chinese conference panel, which included senior officials of Office 610, admitted that members (not only leaders) of the CAG, as soon as they are identified as such, are routinely arrested and sent either to jail or to "reeducation camps" to be "reformed." They insisted that this is justified because the CAG had committed serious crimes.

The Chinese authorities admitted having no evidence for those they arrested, although they had collected "rumors." These included rumors of various riots and accusations of violence and murder in the 1990s, in respect of which Chinese propaganda had circulated photographs of Christian pastors hostile to the CAG allegedly mutilated by CAG members (including one who had an ear cut), and offered "eyewitnesses" to be interviewed by visiting Western anti-cultists and scholars. For these cases, however, there was no evidence that anybody had been prosecuted or sentenced, and no police files or other documents were available, making it impossible to establish any facts beyond the rumors. It is also worth noting that Dunn (2015, 47) reported that she found much clearer evidence in China of violence, including murder, perpetrated *against* the CAG by other Christian groups and movements fearful of CAG's success.

For other cases, however, scholars were directed to documents published by Chinese media and agencies. Thus the 2017 conferences in China allowed for the first time Western scholars to study the crimes allegedly committed by the CAG on the basis of Chinese official documents.

The first and most frequent accusation concerns the Zhaoyuan McDonald's murder of 2014, which I will discuss in detail later. The second most often mentioned case of a crime reputedly committed by members of the CAG happened on August 24, 2013. A woman gouged out the eyes of a young boy named Guo Bin in Shanxi. The boy later became internationally famous for undergoing a successful ocular prosthesis surgery performed in Shenzhen. Folk (2017) carried out an examination of the available sources and concluded that the crime was perpetrated by Guo Bin's aunt, a mentally disturbed person who later committed suicide and had nothing to do with the CAG. In fact Chinese anti-cult sources started associating the crime with the CAG only in June 2014, after the McDonald's murder, and ten months after the local police had closed the case by concluding that the aunt was the sole perpetrator. Folk also learned that accusing Christian missionaries of gouging out the eyes of the Chinese was a common theme in Chinese anti-Christian literature since the nineteenth century. Her study traces the spread of the false accusation that the CAG was involved in the Guo Bin incident from obscure anti-cult websites to a pro-CCP newspaper in Taiwan and then to Western media; it is a fascinating reconstruction of how fake news is fabricated and travels (Folk 2017).

Third, the CAG has also been accused of predicting the end of the world in 2012, within the global framework of the 2012 phenomenon, based on prophecies attributed to the Maya civilization, causing riots and even crimes throughout China. This was another justification used by Chinese authorities to arrest a great number of members of the church. Regarding this case Dunn (2015) wrote that, like many other Chinese, some "members of Eastern Lightning embraced the Mayan prophecy" but they "appear to have done so without sanction from the group's self-proclaimed authorities," who in fact declared Mayan and other theories about the end of the world to be theologically and factually "mistaken." Some of these members were expelled from the CAG (95). Zhao Weishan stated,

"We do not preach the end of the world. . . . The theory of the end of the world is wrong" (The Church of Almighty God 2012b).

Later, Dunn (2016) argued that, while not believing that the world would end in that year, the CAG did try to use the 2012 Mayan fashion as an opportunity for presenting its own views to a larger Chinese audience, but these views were different from the popular end-of-the-world scenarios. As mentioned earlier, the belief that the world would end in 2012 was inconsistent with CAG theology. The church anticipates that some of the predicted catastrophes will occur, but only after the departure of the person the church identifies as Almighty God, who is still on Earth today.

The church also maintains that some flyers and banners depicted on Chinese anti-xie-jiao websites as evidence of its belief in the 2012 prophecies were in fact never part of the materials produced by the CAG. In particular, a brochure was supplied by the Chinese Anti-Cult Association and other Chinese sources to Western media and scholars to "prove" that the CAG had announced the end of the world in 2012. The unsigned brochure (one photocopy of which is in my collection), however, does not mention the end of the world at all, despite its title, *After 2012, the Last Ticket: Gain Salvation in the Catastrophes*. If it has not been fabricated, it must be an example of the literature produced by CAG *dissidents* who resisted Zhao's warnings and, when identified, were promptly expelled.

Dunn (2016, 219) believes that the contested brochure might be authentic, since the same ark drawing appears on another brochure once distributed by the CAG. However, that brochure, *The Church of Almighty God—The Last Ark*, does not mention 2012 at all, nor does it mention theories of the end of the world (The Church of Almighty God 2012a).

Certainly opponents of the CAG resort at times to questionable tactics and produce false documents. In the U.K., for example, a website called Church of Almighty God UK has been created at the address www.chinesetouk.co.uk/. A "Declaration concerning

Websites Imitating The Church of Almighty God" was issued by the church denouncing the site (The Church of Almighty God 2017a).

A fourth example of fake news, which unfortunately played a role in denying asylum to CAG refugees in Europe (see, e.g., Home Office 2017, although the decision was overturned on appeal), is that "a [CAG] member receives 20,000 yuan ($3,237) for every new person they convert" and that new members should pay "2,000 yuan ($323) in membership fees" and spend money buying CAG literature (Mintz 2014).

CAG members interviewed by me and other scholars vehemently deny that this is the case, and given the number of converts, even the richest religious organization in the world would have been quickly bankrupted by giving such money awards for each new convert. The church insists there is no membership fee for any CAG members. As for the literature, the CAG rules mandate that "believers of The Church of Almighty God can enjoy all of the books of God's words, spiritual books, and audio and video productions without charge" (The Church of Almighty God 2017a).

Obviously monetary contributions are needed for a large organization such as the CAG. The CAG's *Principles*, however, allow great latitude on this point:

> Some insist on making an offering of ten percent, while others contribute in different ways. As long as it is being offered willingly, God will gladly accept it. God's house only specifies that those who have only believed in God for less than a year are temporarily exempt from providing any offerings, while poor people are not required to provide any offerings but can make offerings according to their faith. The church will not accept offerings that might lead to family disputes. Those making an offering of money must pray several times, and only after they are sure they are completely willing and are certain they will never have any regrets are they to be allowed to make their offerings. (The Church of Almighty God 2017b, 34)

The derogatory and inaccurate information on fees was spread by the *Newsweek*-associated *International Business Times* in 2014 (Mintz 2014), in an article largely based (and quoting verbatim on this issue) a post-McDonald's laundry list of false accusations against the CAG published by the official newspaper of the Chinese regime, the *People's Daily* (2014).

The McDonald's Case: An Introduction

On May 28, 2014, one of the most horrific murders in the story of new religious movements was perpetrated in a McDonald's restaurant in Zhaoyuan, in the Chinese province of Shandong. Six "missionaries" entered the restaurant preaching their religion and asked clients to leave their phone numbers for further contact. Wu Shuoyan, a sales assistant working in a nearby clothing store, refused to give her number. She was declared an "evil spirit" and beaten to death with a mop handle (Dunn 2015, 204).

Chinese police and media quickly attributed the murder to the CAG, and this accusation is still routinely repeated by international media. As evidence for the accusation, Chinese media reported that, one day after the murder, the police claimed to have found material of the CAG in the home of the main defendant, Zhang Lidong (Chen 2014), including the book *The Scroll Opened by the Lamb* (Phoenix Satellite TV 2014). After another two days, an interview with Zhang was aired on CCTV, China's state television. He stated that he was jobless and that he had killed Wu because she was an "evil spirit." Asked what his religion was, Zhang answered, "Almighty God" (CCTV 2014).

The CAG insists that its literature was probably planted in Zhang's home by the police, but the question does not appear to be crucial. Millions of pieces of CAG literature have been distributed in China, some of them even left "in public locations such as train stations for passers-by to discover" (Dunn 2015, 151). Thus possession of this literature does not prove that one is a member of the church.

There are four Chinese terms the McDonald assassins used for "evil spirit": 邪灵 (evil spirit), 恶灵 (wicked spirit), 恶魔 (demon), and 魔鬼 (devil). They apparently used them as synonymous; at least, from their interviews and declarations at the trial it is unclear whether they made a difference between different categories of "evil spirits." By contrast, the term 恶灵 (wicked spirit), which the group used often, never appears in the vast literature of the CAG, where there are very specific rules for discerning the presence of 邪灵 (evil spirits). Although the CAG, not unlike many other Christian religions, does believe in the existence of evil spirits, it is alien to CAG theology and practice to identify an evil spirit by sight as well as to determine that an evil spirit (or "wicked spirit") must be killed because of its refusal to give out its telephone number.

The group responsible for the McDonald's murder went to trial on August 21, 2014, before the Intermediate People's Court of Yantai, in Shandong province. The Chinese media connected with the government reported quite extensively the statements and confessions by the defendants. From there a story emerged that supported Dunn's conclusion that none of those who entered the McDonald's and were responsible for the crime was, at the time of the murder, a member of the CAG. They were part of a different group, which has never had more than thirty members and which is known only via its connection with the crime. Although Dunn (2015, 204) believes that the assassins, although no longer associated with the CAG at the time of the murder, had once been part of it, I am not persuaded that they were ever members of that church.

The Story of a Micro-Movement

Not a lot is known of the group that was responsible for the Zhaoyuan crime. Most information comes from Chinese government sources and should be approached with caution. However, the main facts are supported by the defendants' statements during the trial and video interviews granted to some Chinese media. The most relevant characters within the group are the Zhang family from Shijiazhuang, in the province of Hebei, and Lü Yingchun, a young woman who was born in Yantai City, Shandong, on March 8, 1975. Zhang Lidong was born on October 8, 1959, in Shijiazhuang. He married Chen Xiujuan, and the couple had three children: two daughters, Zhang Fan, born on October 24, 1984, and Zhang Hang, born on March 1, 1996, and a son, Zhang Duo, born on September 12, 2001 (Wang 2014).

Although she later quarreled with her husband, who had in the meantime acquired a lover, Zhang Qiaolian (born on August 23, 1990), Chen had a relevant part in the genesis of the group's religious interests. She was a member of the Mentuhui, or Association of Disciples, a new religious movement founded by Ji Sanbao in Shaanxi in 1989. Ji, who had been a preacher for the Pentecostal Sabbatarian denomination known as the True Jesus Church, presented himself as "God's stand-in" (*shen de tishen*) and the center of the Third Redemption (Dunn 2015, 35–39).

Lü Yingchun stated at trial, "I grew up knowing that I was 'God Himself.' In 1998, I read the word 'firstborn son' in a book concerning 'Almighty God.' I was convinced that I was the 'firstborn son' myself. . . . Finally, I discovered that I was 'God Himself'" (*Beijing News* 2014).

"Firstborn son" is a title used in the New Testament for Jesus Christ (see Hebrews 1:6; Revelation 1:5). The book Lü refers to may or may not have emanated from the CAG, but certainly in that church there is no God living today on Earth other than the only one they identify as such. Starting in the early 2000s, Lü led a study group in Zhaoyuan. She also spread her messianic claims via the internet.

Zhang Fan confessed that in 2007 she "picked up a copy of the book of 'Almighty God' at our doorstep" and found it persuasive (*Beijing News* 2014). In an interview she said that the book was called *God's Hidden Work* (神隐秘的做功). It is possibly a pirated or imitated version of *The Hidden Work Done by God* (神隐秘的作工), published by the CAG, unless she simply misquoted the title. She did develop an interest in the CAG but never managed to contact the organization: "I never had contact with The Church of Almighty God because they were very secretive, and I could not find them," she later stated (Phoenix Satellite TV 2014).

Zhang Fan's conversion came when she started following Lü on the internet and found her answers to those criticizing her "terrific" (*Beijing News* 2014). She then traveled to Zhaoyuan to hear Lü preaching. Enthusiastic about Lü, in the summer of 2009 she converted her mother and, through her, her whole family, including her father, her sister, and her eight-year old brother. Eventually the whole Zhang family moved to Zhaoyuan, where they rented a two-story building; one story hosted the family textile business and the other the religious gatherings.

Before moving to Zhaoyuan, and after she was admitted in 2002 as a student to the Beijing Broadcasting Institute (renamed in 2004 the Communication University of China), where she would graduate in 2008, Zhang Fan read a book called *The Seven Thunders Sound* (七雷发声; the title refers to the seven thunders or voices describing judgments to come upon the earth in Revelation 10). In Zhaoyuan she found out that the book, which Lü may also have read, had been written by a couple from Baotou, Inner Mongolia: Li Youwang and Fan Bin. At that time Li and Fan were in prison. Zhang Fan borrowed RMB 50,000 from her mother and send them to Baotou so that, upon their release from jail, Li and Fan could move to Zhaoyuan and stay with the Zhang family. Li and Fan "were addressed as 'the two witnesses' [from Revelation 11:3–12] and Lü Yingchun and Zhang Fan were called 'the firstborn sons'" by a group that at that time consisted of twenty to thirty believers (Xiao and Zhang 2014). Another person, Fan Longfeng, became part of the group's inner circle, and in 2010 Lü started living with Zhang Fan.

Some believe that the reference to the "seven thunders" in the apocalyptic visions of Revelation 10:1–7 may indicate a connection with the CAG, but the latter is obviously not the only group with an interest in the Christian Apocalypse and its symbols, and neither the book nor the authors are mentioned in any of the numerous church bibliographies and websites. In fact Voices of the Seven Thunders was the name of a website created in order to *criticize* the CAG, claiming that all of Almighty God's utterances published after 1997 were false (Pan 2015, 191–92). Whether this site had any connection with the book by Li and Fan is unclear; it seems safer to conclude that they operated yet another independent group, although boundaries between different religious movements in the peculiar Chinese situation of persecution and clandestine operations are somewhat porous.

In 2011, however, Zhang Fan pronounced Li Youwang an "evil spirit" (邪灵), and he and his wife left the group in Zhaoyuan and moved to Dongyin, Shandong. Fan Longfeng was also identified as an "evil spirit" (邪灵) and expelled from the group (Xiao and Zhang 2014). With the Li and Fan couple out of the picture, Lü Yingchun and Zhang Fan were free to reveal gradually that they were both the Two Witnesses of the Book of Revelation and God, although full disclosure to their small group might have come only in May 2014.

In the end, as is the case in other Chinese new religions, the core belief of the group was the messianic role of the duo Lü Yingchun and Zhang Fan. The frequent references to the Book of Revelation implied that apocalyptic times were coming, with a final confrontation between good and evil, but those who accepted the divine role of the two young women, "two fleshy bodies sharing a same soul" (*Beijing News* 2014), would be saved. That we live in the last days, Lü explained, was confirmed by the fact that today "people would become 'Satan's' minions unwittingly when they did not understand the situation and would not stand on the side of God. Once that happened, we would be under even greater attack by the 'devil' [魔鬼] during the battle between two spirits" (*Beijing News* 2014).

The messianic role of the duo was exclusive, in opposition to the doctrine of the CAG, which admits only a singular Almighty God. At trial Lü clearly explained, "Only Zhang Fan and I, the 'firstborn sons,' could represent the real 'Church of Almighty God.' Zhang Fan and I are the unique spokeswomen for the real 'Almighty God.' The government has been cracking down on the Almighty God that Zhao Weishan believes in, not the 'Almighty God' we mention. They are fake 'Almighty God,' while we are the real 'Almighty God' " (*Beijing News* 2014).

Zhang Fan added, "Up till now, only my father, my younger brother, my younger sister, Lü Yingchun, Zhang Qiaolian and I are adherents of the real 'Almighty God.' In 2010, I was the 'firstborn son' of 'Almighty God.' I became 'God Himself' because I obtained the authority from the Heaven to kill evil spirits [邪灵] this May. Speaking of 'God Himself,' that is to say, I am God in substance. Lü Yingchun is also God in substance" (*Beijing News* 2014).

Some Christian critics of the CAG believe that it was in the defendants' interest to downplay any relations with the banned organization of Zhao Weishan during the trial, given the Chinese courts' hostility to that church. However, had they adopted a conscious defensive strategy (which they probably didn't), defendants could have claimed that they were not totally responsible of their deeds since they had been manipulated by the CAG; that may have served them better in trying to escape the death penalty for their most serious crime, homicide.

Rather than a branch of one of China's largest new religions, the group was a micro-movement, which never had more than thirty members and was reduced to six in the end (Introvigne and Bromley 2017). Originally Lü Yingchun and Zhang Fan led the group as "shepherds." In the final days of the group, however, Zhang Fan testified that "in the Almighty God organization, Lü Yingchun and I have the highest positions. We are 'God Himself.' My father, younger sister and brother, and Zhang Qiaolian are all the 'chief priests'" (*Beijing News* 2014).

Two elements are worth noting. The first is that no qualification was needed for the priesthood, except the belief in Lü Yingchun and Zhang Fan as Almighty God. Even a thirteen-year old boy such as Zhang Duo was considered a priest. The second is that, contrary to the traditional Chinese family structure, in the Zhang family there was no patriarchal authority or hierarchy determined by age. The father was supposed to obey the daughter without questioning her orders, which completely subverted the traditional family structure.

The Eve of the Crime: The Sad Story of a Dog

Around May 20, 2014, the two "Gods" identified Chen Xiujuan, Zhang Fan's mother, as yet another "evil spirit" and expelled her from the group and from the family home. Then they told Zhang Lidong, Zhang Fan's father, that his marriage with Chen had ended and he could "call his ex-lover Zhang Qiaolian over so that they could live together." Now "they were husband and wife instead [of Chen Xiujuan]. Lü gave them a new spiritual name each. [Zhang Lidong] was called Adam and Zhang Qiaolian, Eve" (*Beijing News* 2014). Zhang Qiaolian, who had not been particularly religious, declared her faith in Lü Yingchun and Zhang Fan as Almighty God and was accepted as a member of the group.

Identifying, denouncing, and expelling evil spirits had become increasingly important for the group. It is a practice with a long tradition in Chinese religion, but Lü Yingchun and Zhang Fan assumed the authority to designate members of their group as evil spirits. Those identified were not simply told to leave: apparently rituals were involved, characterized by increasing violence.

A particularly disturbing episode was the banning from the Zhang family house, and from the group, of Zhang Fan's mother.

Although some could cynically conclude that the move was motivated by the desire to reward Zhang Fan's father, a loyal supporter of the two "Gods," by allowing him to live with his lover rather than with his wife, the expulsion of Chen Xiujuan was enacted as a cosmic drama.

In the days prior to Chen's exile, Lü Yingchun and Zhang Fan announced that they would be "leaving Earth soon" and returning to Heaven. As the expectation for this event grew, so did Zhang Fan's belief that her mother "was the 'king of the wicked spirits' [恶灵之王]. The 'evil spirit' [邪灵] was carrying out its work on us. I would kill my mother when I met her. I was furious after having found out that my mother was an 'evil spirit' [邪灵], and wished upon her a horrible death." Although Zhang Fan did not resort to actual physical violence against her mother, there was a fair amount of symbolic violence. "Words like 'Cruel killing, brutal killing, kill the beasts' were written on the wall in my house. I wrote those words," Zhang Fan confessed (*Beijing News* 2014). Although they also referred to her mother's alleged practice of slaughtering animals, writing them on the walls was an omen of the violence to come.

Actual violence first targeted the family's pet dog, called Luyi, which was identified as "the substitute of Chen Xiujuan" exactly one day before the murder in the McDonald's. Zhang Fan stated, "Over talking, Lü Yingchun noticed that the dog was grinning towards her, which made her think that it was displaying its power and attack. She identified the figure of Chen Xiujuan in the eyes of the dog, which was raised by Chen Xiujuan but was now becoming the tool of the 'demon' [恶魔], the substitute of Chen Xiujuan. . . . Lü Yingchun pointed to the dog and shouted, 'Chen Xiujuan, I've identified you!' . . . In front of the 'demon' [恶魔], we are supposed to dump it or kill it immediately" (Xiao and Zhang 2014).

The episode concerning the dog may seem trivial, but Zhang Lidong devoted to it a significant percentage of his statement during the one-day trial, where he was confronted with the very real possibility of being sentenced to death. "Zhang Fan," he reported, "found

Luyi under the coffee table and took it outside by its tail. She threw the dog onto the floor of the stairway outside the door, and Luyi could not run after that, but crawled instead. Zhang Fan beat the dog with a mop and broke it. The dog stopped moving after a while of beating, but Zhang Fan said, 'Its tail is still moving.' I stepped forward and stomped the dog on its head. It bled profusely after a while of stomping, and I guessed that it was dead. I then dragged it by its tail and threw it into the trash bin outside the building" (*Beijing News* 2014).

Zhang Fan felt that the brutal killing of the dog was an event of religious significance, the confirmation of her divine status. She stated, "On the 26th in particular, on the evening in which the dog was killed, I was even more certain that I and Lü were 'God Himself.' From that evening onwards, I received even greater authority from Heaven and felt especially excited. I had felt that I was God once when I was ten years old, but that was only a thought that flashed in my head for a moment, and I forgot about it after that" (*Beijing News* 2014).

The Murder

It is indeed impressive how, twenty-four hours in advance, the killing of the dog anticipated the killing of the unfortunate salesgirl, Wu Shuoyan. While Zhang Lidong described the goriest details of the murder, it is worth quoting here the account of Lü Yingchun during her confession at trial, since it throws a special light on the spiritual significance of the crime as perceived by the group: "Zhang Hang asked that lady for her phone number, but she refused to give it to her. When I became conscious of it, I found out that we had been attacked and sucked by a 'wicked spirit' [恶灵], which caused us to be weak and helpless. The two of us identified her as that 'wicked spirit' [恶灵], and cursed her with words. Not only did she not listen, her attack got even stronger" (*Beijing News* 2014).

The group saw Wu transfigured into a demon. "We saw the air on her body spiraling her back and tummy. Her tummy bloated, and our spirits sensed that her suction was growing stronger, and so was her attack. My body grew increasingly weaker. In the course of the battle, I saw Zhang Fan falling little by little, as if there was a 'wicked spirit' [恶灵] tugging her downwards. She screamed with all her might, but no sound came out of her mouth. I could only hear a very weak scream." Immediate action was required. "I went to drag her up and she shouted at [her younger sister] Zhang Hang, saying, 'Why did you not believe? Why didn't you move?' I saw Zhang Fan stomping on that woman's head and shoulders after that, and I did the same on her waist and buttocks" (*Beijing News* 2014).

There were no other options: the demon had to die. Unfortunately, to kill the demon it was necessary to kill the salesgirl who hosted it.

> During the attack against us by the "demon" [恶魔], Zhang Fan and I became gradually aware that the woman must die, otherwise it [the demon] would devour everybody. I thus told Zhang Lidong and the rest to beat her up until she stopped breathing. Otherwise, as long as she has breath, the strength of the "demon's" [恶魔] attack on us would not weaken one bit, even if her body was weak and she could not move. I told the people who came to stop us, "Whoever interferes will die." . . . The clash between the woman and us was a battle between two spirits, "God" and "devil" [魔鬼]. The others could not see it, and neither could they understand it. The police could not understand it as well. (*Beijing News* 2014).

A significant detail was that the victim, Wu Shuoyan, was not an opponent of the group. They did not know her until they entered the McDonald's. Her refusal to supply her phone number was, however, perceived as an evil deed of cosmic significance, an unpardonable sin against the duo of Lü Yingchun and Zhang Fan, the self-styled God himself, and the sign that the final battle between "God" and "the demons" had begun.

In the aftermath of the McDonald's murder, which was captured by surveillance cameras and by amateur videos secretly shot by other customers, the Chinese public felt morally shocked by the fact that nobody in the restaurant prevented the murder (see, e.g., the comments by Nancy 2014). The assassins had no weapons; except for Zhang Lidong, four were women and one a child, and they could have been overcome by the other customers. Perhaps they were paralyzed by the extraordinary and sinister performance they were watching.

The whole group, including Zhang Lidong, his daughters, his son, and his lover, and Lü Yingchun, had entered the McDonald's in Zhaoyuan on May 28, 2014. Except for the thirteen-year old Zhang Duo, all were arrested, jailed, and tried by the Intermediate People's Court of Yantai on August 21. On October 11, Zhang Lidong and Zhang Fan were sentenced to death. Lü Yingchun was sentenced to life in prison. Zhang Hang was sentenced to ten years in jail and Zhang Qiaolian to seven years. On February 2, 2015, Zhang Lidong and Zhang Fan were executed.

An apparently inexplicable performance was enacted at the Intermediate People's Court in Yantai on August 21, 2014, and in the jails where the defendants were interviewed. Apart from Zhang Hang, Zhang Fan's younger sister, who declared herself not very religious and with mixed feelings about the whole story (*Beijing News* 2014), none of the other defendants expressed any remorse and did nothing to avoid the harshest penalties. This is particularly surprising for Zhang Lidong, a man in his prime who had been well-off, although he declared himself unemployed, or in full service of his "Gods," at the time of the murder (CCTV 2014).

One explanation may be that Lü Yingchun and Zhang Fan had already announced that they would soon leave Earth and return to Heaven, and that this was part of their divine plan. Execution was simply a way to leave this planet. We can even speculate that Lü would have preferred to share the death penalty with Zhang Fan rather than be sentenced to life in jail. After all, they were "two fleshly bodies sharing the same soul." And Zhang Lidong might simply have wished to join his divine daughter in Heaven.

Conclusion

It is clear that the Chinese government used the McDonald's incident to intensify its persecution of the CAG, even if the church was not responsible of the homicide and the Lü Yingchun–Zhang Fan group was not part of the organization.

The CAG answered by accusing the CCP of having manipulated some "psychopaths" to commit the murder and used it as a justification for cracking down on the church (and, at the same time, on several Christian house churches). "The CCP is the killer and the real sinner" was the accusation on one of the CAG's websites (Eastern Lightning 2015).

Some human rights activists made similar comments. One of them, Xin Shuyan (2014), commented, "After the murder case in Zhaoyuan, Shandong Province, the CCP used the incident to conduct a comprehensive repression on the CAG. It was reported that at least 1,500 innocent members of the Church were arrested. The CCP's campaign-like practice of law enforcement was really a destruction of the rule of law. Why did they carry out the campaign to suppress the 'cult'? There must be ulterior motives. The CCP's intention was simply to conceal the social crisis and to divert public opinion. Thus, they laid blame on the religious groups." (For similar comments, see Guo 2014.) While the CCP's motivations may be interpreted in different ways, it is clear that it did exploit the murder to justify its persecution of the CAG and made it the center of a successful international campaign of fake news. Perhaps serious efforts by scholars to understand what exactly happened in Zhaoyuan in 2014 would lead to a sober assessment of what remains a terrible tragedy.

Or perhaps not. After the scholarly articles were published in 2017, the matter should have been laid to rest. Periodically, however, the CCP tries to revive the dead horse of the McDonald's case (Introvigne 2018e). Zhang Fan was executed in 2015, but Lü Yingchun, who vehemently denied any association with the CAG, is still in jail, and so is Zhang Fan's younger sister, who stated during the trial that she "did not believe very devoutly" (*Beijing News* 2014). Chinese media reported that both were successfully "reeducated" in jail, participated in competitions for the best criticism of *xie jiao*, and were rewarded with sentence reductions. The long articles published by the Chinese media, illustrated by pictures of Lü Yingchun and Zhang Hang denouncing the *xie jiao* before their fellow inmates and participating in jail competitions and performances, are interesting in their own way. They mirror the Western language of deprogramming, yet even after their successful "reeducation" the two women still did not state that they had been members of the CAG (*China News* 2017).

The name Almighty God is repeated obsessively in the articles telling the story of the assassins' "reeducation," with the clear intent of reiterating the association between the McDonald's murder and the CAG. Yet the most the authorities could extract from Lü Yingchun and Zhang Hang after years of intensive deprogramming was that both Lü and the late Zhang Fan had read some CAG books. However, despite her long jail time, Zhang Hang still maintains that their faith was that God had returned to Earth in the dual person of her sister and Lü (Kaiwind Net 2016), a belief obviously very different from the CAG's. Zhang Hang also mentioned that her sister met Lü in "an Internet forum on Almighty God," which was the crucial encounter for the formation of their group (Kaiwind Net 2016). We know, however, from Zhang Fan's trial testimony and interviews that this was a group where Lü spread *her own* messianic claims, which again were clearly incompatible with CAG theology. This means that the "Internet forum on Almighty God" was not related to the CAG.

Lü says she encountered information about the CAG in 1998, yet she maintains that in the same year she was already claiming that she was the "firstborn son of God." She also says that from a "very young age" she realized she "was as perfect as God" (*China News* 2017). In the same article, jail personnel recall that, when she arrived in the prison, Lü expressed her religious beliefs in these terms: "I and Zhang Fan, we have the attributes of God, we are God himself" (*China News* 2017). Certainly these grandiose beliefs about themselves would not have allowed Lü and Zhang Fan to become members of the CAG, and indeed would have been regarded as blasphemous by any CAG member in good standing.

The *China News* (2017) article explains that the "reeducation" of Lü was by no means easy. She collapsed when she learned that Zhang Fan had been executed. It was crucial to the group's faith that "Zhang Fan, who was 'the firstborn son,' would not die and would enter the spiritual world from the flesh." Once again, this belief in the exalted spiritual role of Zhang Fan is not compatible with CAG theology. Zhang Hang had it right when she stated that Lü had "her own theory of 'Almighty God'" (meaning, obviously, one different from the CAG's). Lü believed that she was "the eldest son of God," "the Imperial Son" with absolute authority (although later she became willing to share her divine privileges with Zhang Fan), and ended up building a small "self-contained group" with the few who believed in her claims to divinity (Kaiwind Net 2016).

All this notwithstanding, as late as 2018, while the persecution of the CAG intensified with a massive wave of arrests, the CCP was still trying to attribute the homicide to the CAG by quoting as reliable sources the BBC and other Western media (China Anti-Xie-Jiao 2018), conveniently forgetting that it had fed the fake news to them in the first place. It is an interesting case of "fake news about fake news," showing that, even after several years, the CCP still felt the need to use the McDonald's murder to justify their persecution of the CAG.

7
The Red Dragon and the Pastors
Accusations of Kidnapping

The Red Dragon Strikes Back

In 2017 the international public image of the CAG started changing dramatically. For example, reading the "history" section of Wikipedia on CAG in the main Western languages (something most users of Wikipedia never do) shows how, during 2017, entries on the CAG were regularly updated with references to new articles by scholars. Opponents also updated Wikipedia with news from the Chinese media, but in general the changes resulted in a more balanced assessment. Most academic articles about the CAG available online and offline are now critical of the Chinese government and of its fake news campaigns. In this respect, the conferences against the CAG organized in China in 2017 backfired. Most of the Western scholars who were invited thanked their Chinese hosts for their warm welcome, were grateful for the additional documents they received, but when back in the U.S. or Europe wrote different articles on the CAG from those the Chinese authorities had expected from them (see, e.g., Introvigne 2017a, 2017c, 2018a; Folk 2017). While the Chinese regime was able to enroll some Western scholars in its campaigns against Falun Gong, it was much less successful when it came to the CAG.

CCP anti-cultists did not sit idly contemplating this situation. In the last months of 2017, nearly one hundred articles were published in Hong Kong, Taiwan, South Korea, the United States, the U.K., Russia, and other countries criticizing the CAG and

Inside The Church of Almighty God. Massimo Introvigne, Oxford University Press. (2020).
© Oxford University Press.
DOI: 10.1093/oso/9780190089092.001.0001

reiterating the fake news, ignoring the academic criticism. These articles originated in obscure pro-Chinese media, but occasionally mainline Western newspapers and magazines were persuaded to reprint or quote them.

The first conference against the CAG was held in Henan on June 23–27, 2017. Following the intentions of CCP, the Henan conference should have offered some international academic justification for the persecution, but this did not happen. However, the usual journalistic connections were still working. The church announced that in early July 2017, nearly six hundred CAG members were arrested in Zhejiang Province. The Chinese governmental media did not report the news until July 25, when they claimed that only eighteen members of the CAG had been arrested. On July 27 the Beijing correspondents of multiple foreign media, including the BBC (2017) and *Telegraph* (Connor 2017), reported the arrests, alluding to the old stories about the crimes allegedly committed by the CAG. Some media mentioned the 2012 end-of-the-world riots. I went through all English-language reports of the crackdown published between July 27 and 29, 2017 and found that *all* included references to the McDonald's murder, attributing it to the CAG.

The chronology shows that, after the official Chinese news agency Xinhua (2017) first reported the arrests, the early subsequent coverage was by Sixth Tone (Lam 2017), a website described by *Foreign Policy* as "a media start-up under [Chinese Communist] party oversight that features a slick, attractive website and appealing headlines designed to entice Western readers" (Allen-Ebrahimian 2016). Next came the BBC and the *Telegraph*, some of whose journalists in the Beijing bureaus really seemed to enjoy a special relationship with Chinese propaganda sources, followed by dozens of other media that largely relied on these earlier reports.

The second conference against the CAG was held in Hong Kong on September 15–16, 2017. It too failed to produce an international academic endorsement of the campaign against the CAG. I was among the Western participants, all of whom refused to sign a "final document" with "conclusions" from the conference. I do not claim that media campaigns against the CAG are directly correlated with the conferences. It is possible, however, that the fact that the expected academic support did not materialize was one of the factors persuading the Chinese authorities to launch new campaigns against the CAG through their usual media connections. Another factor may have been that some scholars who had participated in the two seminars, including myself, decided to sign appeals in favor of CAG asylum seekers in South Korea and elsewhere, denouncing the persecution in China, and spoke at international events supporting CAG refugees, including at the United Nations. On October 27, 2017, for example, I appeared at an event organized in Seoul by several NGOs discussing the situation of the CAG refugees in South Korea.

Two days later, on October 30, the Korean daily *Jeju Ilbo* (2017) published an attack against CAG refugees. Some information came from O Myung-Ok, the representative of a Korean pro-Chinese anti-cult magazine, who organized anti-CAG street demonstrations in various Korean cities. Although only a handful of people participated in the demonstrations, they were covered by several Korean media, and the usual accusations were repeated. In the following month, the Hong Kong daily *Ta Kung Pao*, which is owned by the Liaison Office of the Central People's Government in the Hong Kong Special Administrative Region, the agency representing the Beijing government in Hong Kong, published fifteen articles targeting the CAG (see, e.g., *Ta Kung Pao* 2017). Some of their comments were republished by another Hong Kong daily newspaper owned by the same Chinese agency, *Wen Wei Po* (2017), and, quite curiously, by the Taiwan state-owned Central News Agency (Taiwan) (2017). Once again, together with criticism against the CAG refugees in South Korea, the 2012 alleged doomsday predictions and the McDonald's murder were mentioned.

It is in the climate that accompanied and followed the 2017 conferences that Chinese authorities also started mentioning the alleged kidnappings of thirty-four Evangelical Christian pastors and lay leaders in 2002 as one of the most serious crimes allegedly committed by the CAG.

An Evangelical Cliffhanger

The kidnapping incidents were curiously never mentioned by the Chinese authorities before they started interacting with Western scholars. The accusations, however, were directed at the CAG by several Evangelical churches and agencies long before the CCP took an interest in the story. The stories were regarded as believable by several Western Evangelical leaders and media, and even by scholars (Dunn 2015, 154–60), some of whom were later introduced by Chinese authorities during field trips in China to pastors who claimed to have been part of those kidnapped (155). Although there are vague claims, not supported by documents, of other kidnapping incidents involving the CAG (160), the bulk of the accusations concerns a case of 2002, when thirty-four pastors and leaders of the China Gospel Fellowship (CGF) were allegedly abducted and held for two months by the movement. CGF is one of the largest house churches in China; some of its supporters claim that it has some ten million members (Whitaker House 2017).

Having long ignored the accusations and after the CCP propaganda had started mentioning the incident, the CAG published a rebuttal in 2017 noting inconsistencies in the story, finding it strange that nobody was arrested or committed to trial for the crime and that for many years the CCP did not mention the alleged kidnapping at all. The press release concluded that, by inventing the story of the kidnapping, the CGF simply tried to find a justification for the fact that many of its members, including national leaders, had converted to the CAG (The Church of Almighty God 2017c).

True or false, the sensational incident of 2002 proved good material for novels. The American Evangelical novelist C. Hope Flinchbaugh claimed to have visited China and collected firsthand accounts immediately after the kidnapping, which formed the raw material for her novel *Across the China Sky*, published in 2006 with an appendix about what she claims were the "real" facts. In 2017 another novelized account was published, this one by Shen Xiaoming, the leader of CGF, who claimed to have been one of the kidnapped, and the journalist and Evangelical activist Eugene Bach (Shen and Bach 2017).

Well before these books were published, news of the incident "spread like wildfire in Chinese Protestant circles" (Dunn 2015, 157). The kidnappings allegedly occurred on April 16, 2002. After eight days, on April 24, the interdenominational Christian ministry Asia Harvest (2002) started reporting about the incident and posting periodical updates on its website. Almost simultaneously, China Gospel Fellowship started operating a dedicated website, which has been kept alive up to the time of this writing, offering its own day-by-day reports on the kidnapping, requests for prayer, and theological criticism of the CAG (China for Jesus 2002). Together the two sites created a unique instance of an Evangelical cliffhanger.

As told by these sources, and by the later novels, a chronology of the story can be established.

April 28, 2001: Brother Yang, a CGF minister in Pingdingshan, Henan, was contacted by one Ai Yan-Ling, who introduced herself as a house church minister from Yuzhou, Henan. She recommended to Yang a certain Brother Lian, who had just arrived from Singapore, was the brother of Sister Li Shu-Xia, a member of Ai's Yuzhou congregation, and was a good preacher. Not realizing that all these people were members of the CAG, Yang agreed to meet Lian.

April 30, 2001: Brother Yang and his coworker, Brother Jia, traveled to Yuzhou to meet Lian, who introduced himself as the general secretary of Singapore's parachurch Haggai Institute. He suggested that the Institute could train CGF leaders either in China or in Singapore. Lian asked Yang for a CV, phone number, and copy of his ID card to be considered for training. Yang complied and reported back to the leader (and one of the founders) of the CGF, Brother Shen Xiaoming, who asked to meet Lian personally before taking any decision.

June 2001: Yang and Shen together met with Lian, this time in Ying Yang, Henan. They agreed in principle that CGF leaders would receive training from Haggai Institute. However, months passed without Lian calling Yang and Shen to finalize the matter as he had promised.

March 4, 2002: Unexpectedly Lian called Yang after several months of silence. Another meeting with Shen was arranged, where a gentleman who introduced himself as Edward Yu, vice president of the Singapore Haggai Institute, was also present. Yu explained that Haggai had agreed to train thirty-four of the CGF's top leaders in Singapore. He asked for, and later received, their CVs, photographs, addresses, and copies of their ID documents.

April 13, 2002: Yu met with the top leaders of the CGF, including Shen, and explained that, due to the political situation and problems in obtaining passports, Haggai had decided to hold the training in China rather than Singapore, and that the thirty-four CGF leaders would be divided into six groups for training in Shanghai, Zhongxiang (Hubei), Qingdao (Shandong), Renqiu (Hebei), Xi'an (Shaanxi) and Jinzhou (Liaoning). Yu also recommended that CGF trainees not bring their cell phones to the training, as they could be tapped by the authorities.

April 16, 2002: The CGF trainees arrived in the different cities. The teachers, who claimed to be from Singapore and to represent the Haggai Institute, informed them that the security situation had worsened. Those who did not follow the advice and brought their cell phones agreed to hand them over for the sake of security. The six groups were further divided into seventeen groups of two trainees each.

April 17, 2002: Reportedly, except in Shanghai, by this date the CGF trainees realized that the teachers were not from the Haggai Institute but from the CAG. They also said they were confined in the houses where the training was taking place and were not allowed to leave. One Sister Zhao, however, managed to escape.

April 21, 2002: Although some of the top leaders were among those kidnapped, the remaining CGF leaders, alerted by Sister Zhao, convened an emergency meeting and established a crisis unit to deal with the incident.

April 24, 2002: The CGF decided to go public with the story, both through Asia Harvest and its dedicated website, China for Jesus.

April 25, 2002: While aware of the risks involved, the CGF crisis unit decided to send several leaders to Beijing to report to the police what was happening.

April 27, 2002: CGF representatives met the police in Beijing and reported back that they were heard with sympathy and that the authorities promised to help.

April 28, 2002: Two trainees, Brothers Yang and Jing, who were confined in Renqiu (Hebei), managed to escape.

April 30, 2002: According to Asia Harvest, it had "received a confirmed report that after being kidnapped, men dressed in police uniforms came and took the believers away to different places."

May 1, 2002: CGF leaders preached against the CAG in Zhengzhou.

May 7–8, 2002: A national conference denouncing the CAG was convened by the CGF in Zhengzhou.

May 9–10, 2002: Two CGF trainees, Brothers Xing and Qi, were released and reported having been drugged with sexually stimulating substances in order to be seduced by sisters of the CAG.

May 14, 2002: A top leader of the CGF, Brother Zhang, who had been part of the training, was released together with a sister. He reported that the CAG had promised to release all trainees within the next two days.

May 17, 2002: Some of the trainees were released, but not all.

June 3, 2002: Shen Xiaoming and another CGF leader, Shen Yiping, were released.

June 11, 2002: Another two top leaders, Brother Lian and Brother Wei, were released.

June 14, 2002: All remaining trainees were released, except one, who had freely decided to remain with the CAG. CGF-related websites attributed the release to "the forceful pressure" of the police (China for Jesus 2002).

But Was the Story True?

As mentioned earlier, for several years the Chinese authorities and their official media never mentioned the story of the 2002 kidnappings. It became much more famous abroad than in China, where in the following fifteen years it was mostly retold within the CGF and other Evangelical circles. It was only when Western scholars started visiting China to study and discuss the CAG that the Chinese authorities included the story of the 2002 kidnappings in their larger anti-CAG narrative.

I have interviewed Chinese anti-xie-jiao activists, police officers, and pastors of churches hostile to the CAG, as well as members of the CAG, including some who were members of the church in 2002. Based on these interviews, I will now list the arguments advanced in favor of and against the veracity of the CGF narrative. In favor of it, first, the CGF narrative is endorsed by the top leaders of CGF, some of them claiming they had been kidnapped themselves. CGF is a popular group among Evangelicals (Chan and Bright 2005), and its leaders were themselves persecuted by the Chinese regime. Second, a vivid narrative was developed when the events were unfolding: why would it have been invented? Third, according to Dunn (2015, 160), it is true that the CAG's "leadership evidently does not condone the use of violence" (unlike the CGF, Dunn does not believe that the leadership of the church approved or organized the kidnapping), but it is also true that in the situation of persecution it experiences in China, it cannot control the behavior of all its followers. While condemning violence, the leaders "may be unable to impress this upon some followers."

Fourth, Dunn also notes that the CAG itself published the testimony of one "Xie Qiang," which she believes to be a pseudonym for Xue Mingxue, who she states was the thirty-fourth CGF leader "kidnapped," the one who did not come back and decided to join the CAG. Xie Qiang (2015) starts his story as follows: "One day in mid-April 2002, I received a call from my upper leader, and he invited me to Qingdao for a theological training. On the third day of the training, I realized that they were the preachers of Almighty God, the 'Eastern Lightning' sect, as I considered. 'I'm deceived. I'm finished!' I thought to myself, 'If I refuse to accept their way, they will gouge out my eyes or cut off my nose, or even my life will be in danger.'"

However, Xie reports that he was not mistreated or coerced in any way. On the contrary, although he "spoke offensive words to mock or dig at them," the members of the CAG treated him kindly and patiently. "Regardless of how I treated them or what I said to them, they never lost their temper or contradicted me with words but fellowshipped with me patiently. That was just the opposite of my original thought that if I didn't accept their way, I would be in danger, my eyes would be gouged out, my nose would be cut off, and so on." Xie "observed them secretly and found that "their daily prayer before God was sincere, either in the presence of people or behind their backs, which was far more than I could do. They were not like those of an underworld organization at all. Although I didn't listen attentively to their new songs, honestly speaking, both the words and tunes of the songs were very touching." Xie went on to report, "Though I was so unfriendly and arrogant, the host entertained me with warm hospitality all the time. In addition, during the more-than-ten-day stay with them, I found that they were steady and decent and that they kept a very clear distance from the opposite sex and behaved properly in having meals, fellowshipping, and accommodating. There was not at all the 'sexual seduction' as I had fabricated. So, my misunderstanding about the people in this stream gradually disappeared and my resistance against them was also removed" (Xie Qiang 2015). In the end, Xie converted. Dunn (2015, 159–60) speculates that this may be a different, post factum perception of what to other CGF leaders appeared to be kidnapping.

There are other arguments that I believe to be more persuasive, casting doubts on the CGF narrative. In 2002 the CAG was in the midst of a severe persecution in China, with thousands arrested. The main concern of its national and local leaders was to stay out of jail. It is difficult to believe that, hunted by the police, they were able to set up a large-scale kidnapping operation in different cities and provinces.

The CGF was itself persecuted and had survived by going underground (as reported by Shen and Bach 2017 themselves). It is difficult to believe that their members would disclose the names, addresses, and ID card numbers of their top leaders to people they had met only two or three times. The fact that these people had introduced themselves as members of the Haggai Institute should have been a further argument *not* to disclose information to them, as Haggai was known for cooperating with the pro-regime Three Self Church and China Christian Council. In fact the same official CGF account reports that Haggai "had been cooperating with the TSPM (Three Self Patriotic Movement) and CCC (China Christian Council) for a long time" (China for Jesus 2002), without explaining why, nonetheless, CGF leaders trusted Haggai representatives personally unknown to them.

Given the severity of the persecution the CGF was itself experiencing, it is unbelievable that they would run the risk of meeting the police and tell the authorities the names and whereabouts of their leaders. Even less believable is that, faced with a massive cross-province kidnapping, the police did not take any action and did not arrest any member of the CAG—nor of the CGF (itself an illegal group persecuted by the CCP). This would have given further justification to their suppression of the so-called "cults," perhaps following one spectacular anti-cult trial of the kind the Chinese propaganda against the *xie jiao* so cherishes.

Finally, as noted by Dunn (who, as mentioned earlier, believes that the abductions were really organized by rogue members of the CAG, although not condoned by its leaders), kidnapping and mistreating pastors of other churches is against the theology of the CAG. It is also obviously "counterproductive" (Dunn 2015, 160) if the aim is winning the hearts of other Christians and converting them. The CAG may have expelled 300,000 to 500,000 members and, as it stated in its press release, it would have had "no reasons to resort to extreme and bizarre maneuvers to gain some 30 more" (The Church of Almighty God 2017c).

Conclusion

Several scholars have discussed how conversions to "cults" have been consistently interpreted by anti-cultists as "captivity" and "kidnappings" and have proposed comparisons with racist captivity narratives of white Americans (particularly women) captured by Native Americans in the nineteenth century (see, e.g., Bromley 1998; Pike 2009). The captivity narrative of the 2002 incident is unique, however, for the vivid details revealed while the events were allegedly still unfolding. These narratives can be explained in four different ways.

First, one can believe that thirty-four pastors and other CGF leaders were really kidnapped by the CAG, or perhaps, as Dunn would have it, by some members of the CAG who acted against the church's theology and its leaders, who were unable to control them. However, the scale of the operation would have required the coordination of a group of believers large enough to make it virtually impossible to avoid detection.

A second possibility is that real kidnappings were organized by the Chinese police. There is one indication that this is a possibility: Asia Harvest's (2002) "confirmed report" that on April 30, 2002, "after [the CGF leaders had been kidnapped], men dressed in police uniforms came and took the believers away to different places." Asia Harvest did distinguish mere rumors from "confirmed reports" at that time. Of course, the Evangelical organization came to believe that members of the CAG were able to obtain the uniforms and impersonate policemen, but this, given the situation prevailing in China in 2002, is hard to believe. I am personally fascinated by this possibility, although on the other hand I also doubt that Chinese police officers would have been able to teach theology to Evangelical leaders for several days without being unmasked.

The third possibility is that the CGF leaders went to a training to which they were invited (perhaps not under the name of the Haggai Institute) by members of the CAG who did not immediately advertise the name of their church, which some may interpret as deception but can also be explained by the climate of persecution. That CAG members sometimes start missionary conversations or activities in China without disclosing the name of their church has been reported, although it is unclear whether this is a policy set by the leaders for security reasons or a practice individual devotees resort to because of specific local problems.

Only gradually did the CHF leaders realize that they were with the CAG, as reported by Brother Xie Qiang (2015) in his testimony, in which there is no element of violence or kidnapping, according to the common meaning of this term. However, those hostile to the CAG had in the tradition of anti-cult captivity narratives a reservoir of clichés they used to describe their experience (in fact, grossly exaggerating) as kidnapping.

It can also be seen from Xie Qiang's testimony that, already before 2002, to stop their members from converting to Almighty

God, CGF leaders had spread rumors accusing members of the CAG of preaching the gospel through kidnapping and sexual temptation, which greatly impressed their members. The context was one of intense and bitter rivalry between different Christian subtraditions. CGF leaders had to confront a credibility crisis when thousands of their members, including top leaders, converted to the CAG. This is the fourth explanation of how the CGF narrative was generated. Rather than admitting that this was a process they were not able to contain or explain, they invented the kidnapping narrative. This is the interpretation the CAG offered in its 2017 statement (The Church of Almighty God 2017c). Obviously it implies the bad faith of the CGF leaders, whom many describe as honorable men and women. This consideration notwithstanding, it is difficult to escape the conclusion that the narrative they proposed has so many inconsistencies and shortcomings that it cannot be literally true.

Possibly a combination of the third and fourth explanations could be advanced. Some CGF leaders attended seminars or training sessions without realizing they had been invited by the CAG and, although the violence that would justify the label of "kidnapping" was absent, they interpreted their experience in terms of the traditional captivity narratives that were easily accessible to them and part of a Christian tradition of controversies against "cults." This interpretation is supported by conversations other scholars and I had with high-ranking police officers in charge of fighting *xie jiao* in China, who said that in 2002 the incident was not investigated in depth and nobody was arrested.

Others, however, spread the CGF narrative knowing that no kidnappings happened. An academic observer not particularly favorable toward the movement, Chan Kim-kwong (2005), also noted that accusations mentioning the CAG's dishonest techniques of "sheep-stealing" were invoked to explain the loss of members of churches experiencing a phase of decline in an intra-evangelical Chinese religious market that had become increasingly competitive.

There have been other instances in which the CAG has been accused of deceptive methods of proselytization. Some Protestant churches, including the CGF, in the early 2000s circulated an alleged CAG recruitment manual, *Detailed Instructions for Sounding Out and Paving the Way* (摸底铺路细则), which taught members to "infiltrate" Christian churches without initially revealing they belonged to the CAG. The *Sounding Out* controversy escalated to accusations of pressure and violence. Dunn (2015, 147–51) discussed the question and dismissed the stories of violence as largely unbelievable. About the *Sounding Out* manual she considered the hypothesis it was just a fabrication but concluded that it might have been genuine but aimed at resisting persecution rather than deceiving other Christians: "While Protestant and government sources depict 'sounding out' as typifying the general cunning and evil of the movement, the tactic has probably been developed primarily with the goal of protecting vulnerable evangelists, rather than preying upon unsuspecting Protestants" (151). My personal opinion is that the manual includes expressions and refers to practices (such as offering money to win converts) that are not part of the CAG's usual jargon and strategies. Most probably the document was fabricated to slander the CAG by Christian pastors concerned about the high number of conversions to the CAG from their churches, although it may have incorporated sentences copied from genuine CAG material.

On the other hand, the highest administrative leadership of the CAG noticed at one stage that some rogue CAG members did use "low and base means" of evangelization and told them to stop doing so, threatening expulsion. "Practicing an accurate application of God's words to communicate the truth and witness God," the instructions admonished, "is an important principle of evangelism. All those who preach the gospel must strictly comply, in order to conform with God's intentions" (The Church of Almighty God n.d.). And on April 14, 2005, Zhao Weishan instructed, "The gospel must be preached by using regular ways. This has been emphasized many times. Some people still use low and base means to preach the gospel. This must be forbidden. Whoever uses such means to preach the gospel must stop immediately. Anyone who uses them again will be expelled" (The Church of Almighty God 2017b, 68).

When a group believes that its is a unique and urgent message of salvation, based on the very words of God incarnated on Earth, zealous efforts at proselytization normally follow. As the 2005 document illustrates, some members were overzealous; as a result they were disciplined by their leaders. Some Christian critics claim that overzealousness is a unique feature of the CAG and may have involved illegal activities. Overzealous proselytization, however, is common among new religious movements and is not a crime, although it may be annoying to religious competitors. As mentioned earlier, the accusation of "sheep-stealing" is both frequent and understandable when a new movement grows by converting a large number of members of older religions. From early Christians, indeed from the direct followers of Jesus Christ themselves to the first Methodists, such accusations mark the whole history of Christianity.

On the other hand, none of the accusations concerning the use of violence by the CAG for proselytization purposes has been proved. And surely the Chinese authorities, when they started using the kidnapping story in 2017, an incident they had largely ignored for fifteen years, in their campaigns against the CAG, reconstructed it as just one more item of fake news, to be added to the McDonald's murder and the story of the boy whose eyes were gouged out.

8
Escaping China
The Refugees

An International Crisis

Statistics released by the CAG indicate that several thousand refugees have escaped China, particularly after the repression intensified in 2014 using the pretext of the McDonald's murder. In four countries, New Zealand, Canada, Finland, and Sweden, a clear majority of asylum requests have been granted. Elsewhere the majority of requests have not been granted. The numbers I was able to collect from CAG communities in several countries document that the problem of their refugees is now escalating into an international crisis. Note that, in Table 8.1, data for the United States are incomplete, as many refugees there file their applications personally or through local attorneys without reporting to the CAG headquarters.

Apart from a general political and cultural context that may be hostile to refugees in general, and possible Chinese pressure on some Asian countries, particularly South Korea, members of the CAG seeking asylum often encounter problems of differences in interpretation of international conventions (Šorytė 2018) and a lack of reliable information about the CAG and the situation in China.

The Chinese regime is also actively interfering in the cases of asylum seekers, particularly in South Korea. In a typical case, in April 2015 a CAG member called Zhang Fu escaped persecution by moving to South Korea. In May 2016 the CCP ordered Zhang's wife, surnamed Tian, to travel to South Korea with an agent of Chinese

Table 8.1 Asylum Requests of CAG Members as of September 2019

Countries	Total Applications	Asylum Granted	Asylum Rejected	Departure Order	Deported
Germany	310	66	240	14	2
France	444	39	405	236	0
Italy	848	140	343	0	0
Greece	47	7	30	0	0
Netherlands	65	21	26	26	0
Czech Republic	40	3	23	0	0
Finland	39	37	2	0	0
Sweden	9	7	2	2	1
Switzerland	33	2	30	25	3
Portugal	12	0	10	0	0
Belgium	11	0	11	11	0
United Kingdom	8	2	3	0	0
Austria	9	2	7	1	0
Spain	528	0	0	0	0
Australia	233	7	29	0	0
New Zealand	62	53	0	0	0
Saipan	326	3	0	0	0
Japan	274	0	93	0	0
Canada	255	184	25	11	3
South Korea	1023	0	671	180	0
United States	around 1,000	27	1	1	0

Security. They ensnared Zhang into visiting a hotel, and while he was asleep, they took the opportunity to steal his passport and cell phone. They wanted to force him to return to China, but at the last minute he succeeded in a thrilling escape at the airport. In August 2016 and again in November 2017, the CCP sent Tian together with some people of unknown identity to South Korea to create problems for CAG refugees. They contacted the Korean media and insisted that asylum should not be granted to CAG refugees in South Korea (Coordination des associations et des particuliers pour la liberté de conscience et al. 2018). In August and September

2018, and July 2019, South Korean activists against the "cults," led by O Myung-Ok, the representative of a Korean pro-Chinese anti-cult magazine, organized demonstrations in front of different CAG premises in the Seoul area. They were accompanied by Chinese security officers, who had brought with them from China relatives of CAG refugees in Korea, with banners asking them to return home. This was obviously propaganda. Had they agreed to return to China (none of them did), the refugees would not have returned home but would have been taken to jail (Introvigne 2018f).

Six Objections

A cursory examination of the reasons why asylum has not been granted led me to six main reasons. First, CAG is accused of serious crimes, although, as discussed in the previous two chapters, these accusations are either unproven or false. It is also important to note that the individual asylum seekers are not personally accused of any crime.

Second, the authorities may require evidence that the individual has been personally persecuted in China, even though the 2004 *Guidelines on International Protection* for religion-based refugee claims of the Office of the United Nations High Commissioner for Refugees (UNHCR) explicitly affirms that states cannot require evidence that the asylum seeker has been individually persecuted. Although mere membership in a persecuted group is not sufficient, it is enough to prove that the individual has a "well-founded fear of persecution" (United Nations High Commissioner for Refugees 2004, no. 3). It should be abundantly clear to readers of this book that a member of the CAG in China has a very well-founded fear of persecution. If detected, every member of the CAG faces arrest and imprisonment. In December 2018 the Chinese financial newspaper *Caixin Global News* reported that in Qinghai province, "within the past eight months, 1,500 police officers have been deployed in anti-cult projects that target the Church of Almighty God" (Runhua 2018). This massive police mobilization demonstrates that CAG members are mercilessly hunted throughout China.

Although Chinese law itself states that being active in this church is sufficient grounds for being arrested and detained, several countries require evidence that the asylum seeker has been individually persecuted. This creates obvious problems in the case of those who managed to escape *before* being arrested, normally after having been informed by friends in the police that they would be arrested soon. And they will be arrested if they should be compelled to return to China.

Third, some decisions claim that only leaders within CAG are in danger of being persecuted. This is not the case. Article 300 of the Chinese Criminal Code does not distinguish between leaders and common members of groups banned as *xie jiao*, and Chinese case law, as many examples published by Chinese governmental sources show, offers several examples of common CAG believers sentenced under Article 300 (see, e.g., China Judgements Online 2014, 2017; Introvigne, Richardson, and Šorytė 2019).

Fourth, some authorities have objected that the fact that CAG members were able to avoid capture for several years by moving from one city or village to another is evidence that they were not persecuted. But CAG has several million members in China and, like other persecuted religions, has built strong networks of believers capable of operating underground and hiding those brothers and sisters whom the authorities have identified as CAG members. Having to move constantly, without a home and in constant fear of being captured, constitutes precisely the "fear of persecution" specified by the international conventions.

Fifth, a frequent objection is that, as former convicts and/or members of a banned organization, CAG devotees should not have been able to obtain a passport and should have been stopped at the border. The fact that they did leave China and enter another country with a passport was constructed as evidence that they were not persecuted. This objection may seem reasonable, but it ignores the practical realities of the Chinese situation. Chinese authorities claim that there are four million members of the CAG (Ma 2014) and that they have identified and arrested only "several thousands" of them. Even if we accept the figure of 300,000 to 400,000 arrested supplied by the CAG itself (The Church of Almighty God 2017d, 2019c), this would mean that 90% of the members of the church have *not yet been identified* by the authorities. Of course, they can be identified and arrested at any moment or denounced by neighbors interested in obtaining the rewards promised to those who supply information leading to the arrest of a member of a *xie jiao*; accordingly, they live in *fear of persecution*. But as long as they have not been identified, if they do not have a criminal record, they are able to obtain a passport and leave the country.

Once abroad, however, the small communities of the CAG diaspora are easily kept under surveillance by Chinese agents. Unlike in China, most CAG activities abroad are public. They are also often filmed and the videos uploaded to the CAG websites and social network pages. The devotees who are active in the CAG abroad would be immediately arrested should they return to China.

This is confirmed by the case of Li Zhenyuan, a forty-eight-year-old native of Hunchun City, in the province of Jilin, who testified for the Universal Periodic Review of China at the United Nations' Human Rights Council in 2018. On May 18, 2015, Li returned to China from South Korea to renew his visa before it would expire. He believed that the fact that he was a CAG member was unknown to the authorities. However, he was promptly arrested by the police, who showed him photos of performers and audiences from the movies and choir videos produced by the CAG in South Korea, and asked him to identify the persons involved. Li refused, and the Chinese police punched and kicked him, stripped him naked, handcuffed him to the window rails, and deprived him of sleep for six days and nights. Later the police threatened him and his family with dire consequences should Li refuse to return to South Korea and act as an undercover agent, providing them with information about the CAG. Eventually Li pretended to accept their request and seized the opportunity to return to South Korea. Once there he denounced the abuses he had been subject to (Citizens' Coalition for Human Rights of Abductees and North Korean Refugees 2018).

A similar case concerned Yang Shihua, another Chinese member of the CAG, who in early 2018 fled to South Korea due to the increasingly severe persecution in China. But she became seriously sick and flew back to China on May 23, 2018, for medical treatment that was too expensive for her in South Korea. Yang thought that she could pass through customs successfully and that her membership in the banned religion was unknown to the Chinese authorities, as she had kept a low profile in Korea. Unfortunately, she was wrong. She was immediately detained when she landed in Beijing. Her husband, who was waiting for her at the airport, was also detained, though he was later released. Police officers were sent to their home to confiscate laptops, tablets, and cell phones. The incident proves that Chinese authorities keep a close watch on the diaspora communities of banned groups and that members who had not been known as such when they were in China are identified abroad and arrested if they return to China (*Bitter Winter* 2018).

In this respect, refugee boards and courts abroad have been proven tragically wrong in several instances. In 2017 Wang Xiumei, a CAG asylum seeker in Switzerland, received a deportation order from the Swiss authorities (Bundesverwaltungsgericht 2017). They did not believe she was at risk of being arrested in China. Wang agreed to return on May 2, 2017, but she took the precaution of not returning to her home in Linshu County, Shandong, but instead rented a room in the housing facility of a construction company in the same county. Yet on the night of June 27, 2017, the police knocked on her door and arrested her as a member of a *xie jiao*. On February 9, 2018, the Linshu County People's Court (China Judgements Online 2018) sentenced Wang to three and a half years in jail under Article 300 of the Chinese Criminal Code. The verdict made it clear that Wang had been wanted for the crime of "using a *xie jiao*" for having edited and passed to others material of the CAG and having in her possession several CAG books.

Even those members of the church who have been arrested or spent time in jail may still be able to obtain a passport and leave China. Studies by experts of Chinese emigration abroad have concluded that claims in documents supplied by both the Chinese government and NGOs to immigration authorities greatly exaggerate the effectiveness of Chinese systems for collecting data in national databases, fingerprinting, using facial recognition techniques, and performing strict border controls. Data collection and biometrical recognition systems are not fully implemented in the whole immense territory of China and may have technical failures. Controls at the borders are also less strict than these sources claim (Zoccatelli 2019).

And the sources do not consider the prevalence of corruption in China. In 2013 alone, Chinese authorities received the astonishing number of *1.95 million* allegations of corruption (U.S. Department of State 2014). The authoritative *Routledge Handbook of the Chinese Diaspora* (Tan 2012) reports numerous instances of corruption in the issuance of passports to persons theoretically not entitled to one, including members of criminal organizations. Of course, if the officer issuing the passport is corrupt, problems of fingerprints and facial recognition may also be overcome.

Sixth, in some countries asylum seekers were accused of not knowing their religion well enough, so that their very identity as CAG members was in doubt. While useful to determine whether the applicant is a genuine member of the CAG rather than an imposter, interrogations about theology should be consistent with the UNHCR's *Guidelines*, which state that "individuals may be persecuted on the basis of their religion even though they have little or no substantive knowledge of its tenets or practices" (United Nations High Commissioner for Refugees 2004, no. 30).

In some specific cases, asylum seekers' answers did not conform to the tenets of the religion *as depicted in the sources available to immigration authorities*. The sources mentioned, however, were not CAG's normative sacred texts, nor were they part of the scholarly literature. The authorities sometimes relied on media articles that simply translated or repeated Chinese governmental sources. For instance, when church members stated that the McDonald's murder in 2014 was not committed by members of the CAG, they were accused in some countries of not knowing the CAG.

Decisions by immigration authorities and courts in several countries mention an old report from the Immigration and Refugee Board of Canada (2014b) that, although it is not a UNHCR document, is available on the UNHCR database. The Canadian Board did considerable homework, but the report is dated 2014 and was written before the flourishing of academic studies on the CAG in 2017–18. It was thus largely influenced by Western media articles that simply repeated the Chinese propaganda and includes significant factual mistakes, as did other documents by the Immigration and Refugee Board of Canada (2013 [an earlier and less accurate version of 2014b], 2014a). A parallel document published in 2016 by French authorities was largely a compilation of Chinese governmental sources, often presented in a style and language typical of the anti-cult movement (Division Information Documentation Recherches 2016). Interestingly, the Canadian documents did not seem to play a significant role in Canada, where the large majority of asylum applications by members of CAG (so far, 184 out of 255) have been accepted. Hopefully, this may soon become a problem of the past, since in 2019 Canada and other countries moved to produce more updated information about the CAG, based on interviews with Western scholars who have recently studied the church.

Another source of problems for CAG asylum seekers is due to members referring to the incarnate Almighty God as "he" rather than "she," despite believing that Almighty God is a woman, and because they never mention the civil name of God's incarnation (as they say, out of reverence for God). This has created misunderstanding and suspicion in their interviews with immigration authorities.

It is of course possible to falsely claim to be a member of the CAG, although the church has developed an effective system for communicating with its underground communities in China and determining who is a bona fide member. In most diaspora countries, there are incorporated local bodies able to certify who is a member and who is not. There should be no reason to reject asylum requests by certified CAG members. Their status as members of the CAG is enough to justify a "credible fear of persecution" and, should they be compelled to return to China, they would be arrested and sentenced to long jail terms, or worse.

Happily, at least in some countries, as refugee boards and courts become more familiar with the scholarly literature on the CAG, the situation is slowly improving (Calvani 2018, 2019). In Italy, for instance, although the total number of negative asylum decisions is still higher than those favorable to the CAG refugees, most of the positive decisions have been rendered recently.

9

Some Conclusions

The Church of Almighty God in Xi Jinping's China

Mao Zedong established his Communist regime in China in 1949. Some of his writings about religion remain classified to this day, but those that have been published are enough to distinguish between two different periods in his attitude toward believers. Despite occasional propaganda arguing otherwise, there is little doubt that Mao was fully committed to atheism and the total eradication of religion. However, when the CCP first rose to power, Mao believed that an immediate, severe, and indiscriminate persecution of all religious believers was neither appropriate nor necessary. It was not appropriate, as it would have had catastrophic effects on the image and international relations of the newly established Communist regime. And it was not necessary because Mao, as a dogmatic adherent to classic Marxist-Leninist philosophy, was firmly convinced that, as a Communist society and lifestyle were implemented in China, religion would disappear slowly and spontaneously, having lost the social roots it needed to survive (Yang 2006).

This does not mean that Mao simply left religion alone. He believed the process of its gradual extinction should be accompanied, governed, and accelerated by the CCP, and he undertook four major measures to implement this policy. First, he expelled all foreign missionaries. Second, he recruited believers sympathetic to the CCP as fellow travelers to create five CCP-controlled associations, into which he believed all religious communities should be incorporated: the Protestant Three Self

Church (1954), the China Buddhist Association (1953), the China Islamic Association (1953), the China Taoist Association (1957), and the China Catholic Laity Patriotic Committee (1957), later renamed the Chinese Patriotic Catholic Association, or the Patriotic Catholic Church, separated (until 2018) from the Vatican.

Third, he tightened control on Muslims in Xinjiang and, after he invaded Tibet in 1950, on Buddhists in that country. As modern scholars have demonstrated, Mao severely persecuted Tibetan Buddhists living in regions of China other than Tibet and, when Tibetans in Tibet protested, he used their protests as a pretext to impose a regime of persecution there (Li 2016). Fourth, he continued the imperial and republican policies against new religious movements classified as *xie jiao*. The massive persecution of Yiguandao was a case in point.

Mao's measures did not work. As the Communist regime was being implemented and consolidated, religion showed no signs of disappearing. On the contrary, it flourished, and its most vital and growing segment was constituted by Christian house churches and movements that stubbornly remained outside the government-controlled Three Self Church. Historians have firmly established that, since the "soft" methods had failed, eradicating religion through violence was one of the main aims of the Cultural Revolution, and that Mao, rather than being manipulated by others, was the main instigator of the Cultural Revolution and its atrocities (MacFarquhar and Schoenhals 2006).

During the Cultural Revolution, between 1966 and 1976, all religious communities and institutions were liquidated, including the five authorized religions established and controlled by the CCP. Countless temples, churches, and mosques were destroyed, and an important part of China's spiritual, artistic, and cultural patrimony perished forever. Even keeping a Bible or a statue of Buddha in the home was enough to be arrested and, in several cases, executed. At least half a million believers, possibly many more, were either executed or died in labor camps. In the early 1970s the Red Guards announced that religion in China had been "wiped away like dust" (Yang 2006, 101).

Chairman Mao died in 1976, and Deng Xiaoping rose to power in 1978. Deng quickly put an end to the Cultural Revolution, realizing that it was destroying not only Chinese culture and monuments but the Chinese economy and the regime itself. Deng's interpretation of the Cultural Revolution as a catastrophic mistake remains the official orthodoxy to this day. One thing the Cultural Revolution had not destroyed, however, was religion. When the dust settled, it became clear that, although thousands of believers had been killed, religion had survived underground.

Deng was not a critic of Communism, but he came to the conclusion that religion's demise would require centuries, not years or decades. In 1982 he enacted *Document 19*, restoring the five authorized religions to their pre–Cultural Revolution status (Yang 2004). Deng even tolerated a gray market of unauthorized religions—with limits: the Shouters, for example, were declared a *xie jiao* and banned in 1983, only one year after *Document 19*—and encouraged traditional practices such as *qi gong* as being cultural rather than religious. Deng's system of limited tolerance should not be confused with religious liberty. The Underground Catholic Church and several house churches continued to be persecuted, and the propaganda urging acceptance of scientific atheism did not stop. However, the Deng era was, comparatively speaking, a less severe time for religion in Communist China. Some scholars believe that the Deng era continued with his successors, until Xi Jinping acceded to power in 2012 (Meng 2018).

But the situation gradually worsened even before Xi. There was a subtle shift from *Document 19*'s formula of "subjecting religion to socialist education" to the wording prevailing in documents of the 1990s, "actively guiding religion to adapt to socialist society," which was reflected in new regulations enacted in 2004 and 2005 (Meng 2018, 49). Three events marked a worsening of the situation for religion in China in the period between the repression of the

Tiananmen Square protest in 1989 and Xi's accession to the position of CCP secretary in 2012. The first event was the terrorist attack on the United States on September 11, 2001, which offered the CCP the pretext to crack down on Muslim Uyghurs and other ethnoreligious Muslim minorities, claiming, falsely, that a very significant number of them supported terrorism. (Although some did, they were a tiny minority.) The second was the renewed crackdown on *xie jiao* from 1995 on. This was mostly due to the unexpected success of Christian new religious movements, the largest of which was the CAG. Since 1995 the list of *xie jiao* became the main tool of a massive persecution, reminiscent of the suppression of Yiguandao in the 1950s. Third, in 1999 the CCP clashed with Falun Gong, with which it had maintained a good relationship for several years as part of the tolerance and promotion of *qi gong*. Falun Gong was listed as a *xie jiao*, and its persecution was extreme in terms of both scope and cruelty.

Xi Jinping became secretary of the CCP in 2012 and president of China in 2013. The term "neo-Maoism" is sometimes used to describe his ideology, but the term should be handled with care, since Xi never denied that the Cultural Revolution had been a disaster for the country, nor did he overturn the economic pro-capitalist reforms of his post-Mao predecessors. However, Xi exhibited some similarities with Mao in reinforcing the position of the CCP secretary, promoting the cult of his own (and, occasionally, Mao's) personality, and cracking down on religion.

A careful study of Xi's pronouncements and policies on religion shows very clearly that he believes that too much latitude had been given to the development of religion in China since Deng. This led to an unprecedented growth of house churches and, worse still, of *xie jiao* such as the CAG. Although his predecessors had already acted against *xie jiao* with ferocity, greatly reducing the presence of Falun Gong (but not of the CAG) in China, Xi took new measures to crack down on *xie jiao*, using violent language reminiscent of the anti-Yiguandao campaigns of the 1950s. Times having changed since the 1950s, however, Xi's CCP also promoted a massive campaign of fake news aimed at justifying the persecution internationally, enrolling anti-cultists (some of them Christian) and journalists in Asia and the West as fellow travelers. The false accusation that the CAG was responsible for the McDonald's murder of 2014 (in fact, as we have seen, perpetrated by another religious movement) was a spectacular example of Xi's international campaign of fake news.

Xi lost patience with Deng's strategy of accompanying religion to a slow demise through a process that would last for decades or even centuries. He decided to act decisively against all three segments of the Chinese religion. The official CCP-controlled five authorized religions had to understand that they existed to administer the demise of religion, not to promote it. Xi ordered the strict enforcement of provisions forbidding minors to enter churches or temples or to be subject to any form of religious education, hoping this would prevent the transmission of religion to new generations. Xi increased to record numbers those arrested, detained, and killed in campaigns against Uyghurs and other Muslim minorities in Xinjiang, dissident Buddhists in Tibet, and *xie jiao*. Those members of Falun Gong who still remained in China were again mercilessly hunted, but Xi's greatest wrath was reserved for the CAG, as his specialized anti-xie-jiao police told him, perhaps exaggerating the figures, that, despite the repression, the church was still growing and by 2014 had reached the spectacular number of four million members.

In 2018 Xi's policy on religion was institutionalized with the coming into force of the New Regulation of Religious Affairs. Xi's main aim became clear. Between the five authorized religions and the banned *xie jiao* lies the so-called gray market that includes most Chinese believers (Aikman 2005; Vala 2018). They attend the Protestant house churches, the Underground Catholic Church (a problem Xi tried to solve with the agreement China signed with the Vatican in 2018), and a plethora of Muslim, Buddhist, and Daoist organizations, mosques, and temples that are not part of the official associations.

The core message of the new law, whose full implementation awaits further regulations, is that the relative and limited tolerance this gray market has enjoyed since Deng's *Document 19* is coming to an end. The house churches and independent mosques and temples are told that they must either join the official associations of the five authorized religions or they will be persecuted and relegated to the hell of the *xie jiao*. In the second half of 2018, legal scholars started noticing an alarming phenomenon: judges were applying Article 300 of the Chinese Criminal Code, which makes it a crime to be active in a *xie jiao*, against believers whose communities are *not* listed as *xie jiao* yet are not part of the five authorized religions either.

Places of worship of the gray market religions—churches, mosques, Buddhist and Daoist temples—as well as crosses and statues of Buddha and Lao-Tzu are being destroyed. Some places of worship of the five authorized religions are also occasionally demolished, using as pretexts violations of zoning regulations or that minors have been allowed inside.

Still, it is doubtful that the gray market will be completely eliminated. In a recent book about Chinese Protestants, Carsten T. Vala (2018) observes that the CCP is ill-equipped to deal with thousands of house churches and, so far, the repression has been conducted selectively. Only those house churches have been persecuted that have crossed certain unwritten "red lines," which mandate that they should remain small (the rise of urban megachurches is one of the causes of the new restrictions) and local (national organizations and networks are not tolerated), not invite foreign preachers, allow the authorities to keep a watch on their activities, and avoid any criticism of the CCP and the Three Self Church. Although Vala's book does not deal with the *xie jiao*, he takes it for granted that another red line not to be crossed is "orthodoxy." Both Three Self and house churches are expected to firmly denounce "heterodox teachings," and they are generally not unwilling to do so, as they perceive the active proselytizing by Christian *xie jiao* as a form of unfair (but successful) competition. Paradoxically, an officially atheistic regime would use a certain interpretation of Christian theology to decide which religious groups should be suppressed. For the CCP, this provides a convenient rationale to justify its suppression of fast-growing independent religious groups. If spaces of tolerance are shrinking for house churches, they never existed for the *xie jiao*.

Xi Jinping faces a growing international public relations problem. Fake news is still occasionally believed about *xie jiao* such as Falun Gong and the CAG, but most Western scholars increasingly offer alternative narratives challenging the propaganda. International protests denounce the massive detention of Muslim Uyghurs in jail-like "transformation through education" camps. Falun Gong continues its international public campaigns denouncing the CCP, and a coalition of human rights activists, scholars, and NGOs protesting the persecution of the CAG is gaining momentum, something the CCP did not expect.

This book has described the growth and persecution of the CAG in the present Chinese context but does not offer previsions for the future. Some may believe that ultimately the work of scholars and human rights activists will persuade the Chinese authorities that their campaigns against the CAG and other groups banned as *xie jiao* are both unnecessary and detrimental to China's international image. I am more pessimistic. Ultimately, eradicating the *xie jiao* and any other group perceived as hostile to the CCP seems to be a more important goal for Xi than improving the controversial human rights image of his regime.

References

Aikman, David. 2005. *Jesus in Beijing: How Christianity Is Transforming China and Changing the Global Balance of Power.* Oxford: Monarch Books.

Allen-Ebrahimian, Bethany. 2016. "China, Explained." *Foreign Policy,* June 3. http://foreignpolicy.com/2016/06/03/china-explained-sixth-tone-is-chinas-latest-party-approved-outlet-humanizing-news/.

Ann. 2017. "Behold! The Scroll Has Been Opened!—Return to God." Find the Shepherd, October 12. https://www.findshepherd.com/behold-the-scroll-has-been-opened.html.

Anthony, Dick. 1996. "Brainwashing and Totalitarian Influence: An Exploration of Admissibility Criteria for Testimony in Brainwashing Trials." PhD diss., Graduate Theological Union, Berkeley.

Anthony, Dick, and Massimo Introvigne. 2006. *Le Lavage de cerveau: Mythe ou réalité?* Paris: L'Harmattan.

Asia Harvest. 2002. "When China's Christians Wish They Were in Prison." Accessed December 17, 2017. https://asiaharvest.org/when-chinas-christians-wish-they-were-in-prison.

Barker, Eileen. 1984. *The Making of a Moonie: Choice or Brainwashing?* Oxford: Basil Blackwell.

BBC News. 2017. "Chinese Police Detain 'Female Jesus Cult' Members." July 27. http://www.bbc.com/news/world-asia-china-40737430.

Beijing News. 2014. "山东招远血案被告自白:我就是神" (The Confession of the Defendant of the Murder Case in Zhaoyuan, Shandong: "I am God Himself"). August 22. Compiled by Yang Feng. https://web.archive.org/web/20190815034427/http://news.sina.com.cn/c/2014-08-22/123730728266.shtml.

Bitter Winter. 2018. "Church of Almighty God Refugee Arrested upon Her Return to China." June 5. https://bitterwinter.org/church-of-almighty-god-refugee-arrested-upon-her-return-to-china/.

Bromley, David G. 1998. "The Social Construction of Contested Exit Roles: Defectors, Whistleblowers, and Apostates." In *The Politics of Religious Apostasy: The Role of Apostates in the Transformation of Religious Movements,* edited by David G. Bromley, 19–48. Westport, CT: Praeger.

Bundesverwaltungsgericht. 2017. "A. gegen Staatssekretariat für Migration." Decision of January 23, E-7624/2016. Accessed January 28, 2019. https://jurispub.admin.ch/publiws/download?decisionId=9bcf92dd-e5b0-4ae7-aa4d-323b464340de.

Calvani, Cristina. 2018. "I cinesi richiedenti asilo in Italia per motivi religiosi: La Chiesa di Dio Onnipotente." MA thesis, University of Perugia.

Calvani, Cristina. 2019. "Religion-Based Refugee Claims in Italy: Chinese Asylum Seekers from The Church of Almighty God." *Journal of CESNUR* 3(3):82–105. doi:10.26338/tjoc.2019.3.3.4.

CCTV. 2014. "招远案杀人嫌疑犯采访全程-我感觉很好 全能神教的信徒" (Oriental Horizons, The Whole Process of Interview with the Suspect of the May 28 Zhaoyuan Murder Case: "I Feel Pretty Good"—Adherent of the Group of Almighty God). May 31. https://web.archive.org/web/20190911033550/https://video.sina.cn/news/i/2014-05-31/detail-icfkptvx2559576.d.html?from=wap.

Center for Religious Freedom. 2002. "Report Analyzing Seven Secret Chinese Government Documents." February 11. https://www.hudson.org/content/researchattachments/attachment/566/analysis_of_china_docs_1_to_7.pdf.

Center for Studies on Freedom of Religion Belief and Conscience and Association for the Defense of Human Rights and Religious Freedom. 2018. "Universal Periodic Review, China. Religious Freedom in China: The Case of The Church of Almighty God." Submission to the United Nations' Human Rights Council. Accessed December 1, 2018. https://uprdoc.ohchr.org/uprweb/downloadfile.aspx?filename=5576&file=EnglishTranslation.

Central Committee of the Chinese Communist Party. 1982. "Document 19: The Basic Viewpoint on the Religious Question during Our Country's Socialist Period." English translation. Accessed April 26, 2018. https://www.purdue.edu/crcs/wp-content/uploads/2014/08/Document_no._19_1982.pdf.

Central News Agency (Taiwan). 2017. "港媒：受陸禁教派在港招攬大陸新移民" (HK Media: Sect Banned by Mainland China Now Recruiting New HK Immigrants from Mainland). November 20. http://www.cna.com.tw/news/acn/201711200058-1.aspx.

CESNUR. 2017. "La Chiesa di Dio Onnipotente—'Lampo da Levante.'" In *Enciclopedia delle Religioni in Italia*. Accessed April 11, 2018. http://www.cesnur.com/la-chiesa-di-dio-onnipotente-folgore-da-oriente/.

Chan Kim-kwong. 2005. "A New Messiah from China: The Church of the Almighty God (Eastern Lightning Sect)." Paper presented at the 19th World Congress of International Association for the History of Religions, Tokyo, March 29.

Chan, Lois, and Steve Bright. 2005. "Deceived by the Lightning." *Christian Research Journal* 28:3 (online edition). http://www.equip.org/article/deceived-by-the-lightning.

Chen, Lu. 2014. "Questions Raised over Violent Killing in China McDonalds." *Epoch Times*, June 1. http://www.theepochtimes.com/n3/709284-questions-raised-over-violent-killing-in-china-mcdonalds.

Chen, Qingping. 2017. "Reflection on the Definition of Cults and Its Related Problems." Paper presented at the conference The Question of Xiejiao in

China and the Case of the Church of Almighty God, University of Hong Kong, September 15–16. Manuscript in the conference booklet.

Chen, Wei, Yin Junxiu, and Wu Tong, dirs. 2017. *Red Re-Education at Home*. Seoul: Olive Leaf Film Studio. Accessed February 7, 2018. https://www.holyspiritspeaks.org/videos/red-re-education-at-home-movie/.

China Anti-Xie-Jiao. 2018. "境外主要媒体关注中国依法处决招远邪教杀人案主犯" (Prominent Media outside Border Concerned with the Main Criminals of Zhaoyuan Cult Murder Executed in China Pursuant to the Law). May 22. http://www.chinafxj.cn/bgt/jtxjqns/llqm/201502/16/t20150216_9560.shtml.

China for Jesus. 2002. "Report from China Gospel Fellowship of the April 16 Kidnapping by the Eastern Lightning Cult." Accessed April 24, 2018. http://chinaforjesus.com/cgf/070702/index.htm.

China Judgements Online. 2014. Case of July 31, 2014 (Sun Teng). Accessed September 11, 2019. http://wenshu.court.gov.cn/website/wenshu/181107ANFZ0BXSK4/index.html?docId=d7b3c32dda9c4048b4140b4c646f8bc2.

China Judgements Online. 2017. Case of January 23, 2017 (Xie Guangsheng). Accessed September 11, 2019. http://wenshu.court.gov.cn/website/wenshu/181107ANFZ0BXSK4/index.html?docId=b196d7f7f00a4e72bc41a7eb010465ad.

China Judgements Online. 2018. Case of February 2, 2018 (Wang Xiumei and Zhang Delan). Accessed September 9, 2019. http://wenshu.court.gov.cn/website/wenshu/181107ANFZ0BXSK4/index.html?docId=3ecaf29352574dffa10da8a200aff7f4.

ChinaNews. 2017. "招远麦当劳杀人案女犯忏悔记：两年写几万字揭批材料" (Confession by the Main Criminal of Zhaoyuan McDonald's Murder: Having Compiled Materials of Revelation and Criticism Amounting to Tens of Thousands Chinese Characters in Two Years). Sourced from *China Youth Daily*. May 26. http://www.chinanews.com/sh/2017/05-26/8234450.shtml.

Christopher. 2016. "A Pastor's Spiritual Confession." Find a Shepherd, September 9. https://www.findshepherd.com/a-pastor_s-spiritual-confession.html.

The Church of Almighty God. N.d. "Principles of Spreading the Gospel and Bearing Testimony to God." In *Practice and Exercises for Principled Behavior*. Accessed March 31, 2019. https://en.godfootsteps.org/principles-of-spreading-the-gospel-and-bearing-testimony-to-god.html.

The Church of Almighty God. 2012a. *The Church of Almighty God—The Last Ark*. N.p.: The Church of Almighty God.

The Church of Almighty God. 2012b. "给各地教会神选民的一封信." (A Letter to God's Chosen People of All Churches). December 16. https://www.hidden-advent.org/inst/20121216.html.

The Church of Almighty God. 2015. "A Brief Talk about 'The Millennial Kingdom Has Arrived.'" Accessed April 11, 2018. https://www.holyspiritspeaks.org/a-brief-talk-about-the-millennial-kingdom-has-arrived/.

The Church of Almighty God. 2017a. "Declaration Concerning Websites Imitating The Church of Almighty God." February 24. https://www.holyspiritspeaks.org/solemn-declaration/.

The Church of Almighty God. 2017b. 全能神教会历年工作安排精要选编（实用本）[Selected Annals of the Arrangements of the Work of The Church of Almighty God (Practical Version)]. Seoul: The Church of Almighty God.

The Church of Almighty God. 2017c. "Statement: The Church of Almighty God Did Not Kidnap 34 Leaders of China Gospel Fellowship in 2002. The Kidnapping Incident Is Simply a Fabrication." October 18. https://www.holyspiritspeaks.org/statement/.

The Church of Almighty God. 2017d. *2017 Annual Report on the Chinese Communist Government's Persecution of The Church of Almighty God*. Seoul: The Church of Almighty God. http://www.cesnur.org/2017/almighty_china_report.pdf.

The Church of Almighty God. 2017e. *The Word Appears in the Flesh*. Seoul: The Church of Almighty God.

The Church of Almighty God. 2018a. "Chapter 26: How to Transition Into the New Age" *Records of Christ's Talks*. Accessed September 9, 2019. https://en.godfootsteps.org/into-the-new-age.html.

The Church of Almighty God. 2018b. "Focusing on Solving Three Problems That Are Currently Widespread in the Church." *Classic Selections from Sermons and Fellowship on Entry into Life*. Accessed March 16, 2018. https://www.holyspiritspeaks.org/chapter-82-focusing-on-solving-three-problems/.

The Church of Almighty God. 2018c. Introduction [to *The Word Appears in the Flesh*, not included in the printed English version]. Accessed November 3, 2018. https://www.holyspiritspeaks.org/introduction-word/.

The Church of Almighty God. 2018d. "None Who Are of the Flesh Can Escape the Day of Wrath." *Utterances of Christ of the Last Days (Selections)*. Accessed April 26, 2018. https://www.holyspiritspeaks.org/none-who-are-of-the-flesh-can-escape-the-day-of-wrath-2/.

The Church of Almighty God. 2018e. *The Secret of the Wise Virgins. Listen to the Voice of God. Behold the Appearance of God*. Seoul: The Church of Almighty God.

The Church of Almighty God. 2019a. *The Appearance and Work of Almighty God: The Origin and Development of The Church of Almighty God*. Booklet of the Exhibition. The Appearance and Work of Almighty God: The Origin and Development of The Church of Almighty God, Seoul, Onsu Church of Almighty God, 24 October 2018-(ongoing). Seoul: The Church of Almighty God.

The Church of Almighty God. 2019b. "Chapter 95" [of *The Word Appears in the Flesh*, not included in the printed English edition]. Accessed April 21, 2019. https://en.godfootsteps.org/the-ninety-fifth-utterance.html.

REFERENCES 137

The Church of Almighty God. 2019c. *The Chinese Communist Government's Persecution of The Church of Almighty God: Annual Report 2018*. Seoul: The Church of Almighty God. Accessed March 28, 2019. https://www.adhrrf.org/wp-content/uploads/2019/02/EN-annual-report-2018.pdf.

Citizens' Coalition for Human Rights of Abductees and North Korean Refugees. 2018. "Universal Periodic Review, China. Submission: Protection of Civil and Political Rights." Submission to the United Nations' Human Rights Council. Accessed December 1, 2018. https://uprdoc.ohchr.org/uprweb/downloadfile.aspx?filename=5718&file=EnglishTranslation.

Connor, Neil. 2017. "China Detains 18 Members of 'Cult' Which Believes Jesus Was Reincarnated as a Woman." *The Telegraph*, July 27. https://www.telegraph.co.uk/news/2017/07/27/china-detains-18-members-cult-believes-jesus-reincarnated-woman/.

Coordination des associations et des particuliers pour la liberté de conscience, Center for Studies on New Religions, European Interreligious Forum for Religious Freedom, European Federation for Freedom of Belief, and International Observatory of Religious Liberty of Refugees. 2018. "Universal Periodic Review, China. Religious Freedom and Persecution in China: The Case of The Church of Almighty God." Submission to the United Nations' Human Rights Council. Accessed December 1, 2018. https://uprdoc.ohchr.org/uprweb/downloadfile.aspx?filename=5513&file=Cover Page.

Davis, David Brion. 1960. "Some Themes of Counter-Subversion: An Analysis of Anti-Masonic, Anti-Catholic, and Anti-Mormon Literature." *Mississippi Valley Historical Review* 47(2):205–24.

Division Information Documentation Recherches. 2016. *L'organisation millénariste Almighty God*. Paris: DIDR.

Dunn, Emily. 2008a. "The Big Red Dragon and Indigenizations of Christianity in China." *East Asian History* 36:73–85.

Dunn, Emily. 2008b. "'Cult,' Church, and the CCP: Introducing Eastern Lightning." *Modern China* 35(1):96–119.

Dunn, Emily. 2010. "Heterodoxy and Contemporary Chinese Protestantism: The Case of Eastern Lightning." PhD diss., University of Melbourne.

Dunn, Emily. 2015. *Lightning from the East: Heterodoxy and Christianity in Contemporary China*. Leiden: Brill.

Dunn, Emily. 2016. "Reincarnated Religion? The Eschatology of the Church of Almighty God in Comparative Perspective." *Studies in World Christianity* 22(3):216–33. doi:10.3366/swc.2016.0157.

Dunn, Emily. 2018. "Quánnéngshén Jiàohuì (Dōngfāng Shǎndiàn)." In *Handbook of East Asian New Religious Movements*, edited by Lukas Pokorny and Franz Winter, 504–23. Leiden: Brill.

Eastern Lightning. 2015. "An Extensive Exposure to the Sinister Intention of the Evil CCP's High-Profile Public Trial on the Psychopaths." October 16.

Accessed April 24, 2018. https://easternlightning.wordpress.com/2015/10/16/an-extensive-exposure-to-the-sinister-intention-of-the-evil-ccps-high-profile-public-trial-on-the-psychopaths-2/. No longer available.

Elliott, Mark C. 2001. *The Manchu Way: The Eight Banners and Ethnic Identity in Late Imperial China*. Stanford, CA: Stanford University Press.

Fang, Yuwei. 2011. "從入會至癡迷—對基督教異端"全能神"教成員卷入的社會學研究" (From Conversion to Fanaticism—The Sociological Research on Members Involved in the Christian Heresy "Almighty God"). MA thesis, Shandong University.

Flinchbaugh, C. Hope. 2006. *Across the China Sky*. Minneapolis, MN: Bethany House.

Folk, Holly. 2017. "'Cult Crimes' and Fake News: Eye-Gouging in Shanxi." *Journal of CESNUR* 1(2):96–109. doi:10.26338/tjoc.2017.1.2.5.

Folk, Holly. 2018. "Protestant Continuities in The Church of Almighty God." *Journal of CESNUR* 2(1):58–77. doi:10.26338/tjoc.2018.2.1.4.

Gallagher, Eugene V., ed. 2016. *"Cult Wars" in Historical Perspective: New and Minority Religions*. New York: Routledge.

Gelfert, Axel. 2018. "Fake News: A Definition." *Informal Logic* 38(1):84–117. doi:10.22329/il.v38i1.506.

Goossaert, Vincent, and David A. Palmer. 2011. *The Religious Question in Modern China*. Chicago: University of Chicago Press.

Gracie, Carrie. 2014. "The Chinese Cult That Kills 'Demons.'" *BBC News*, August 13. http://www.bbc.com/news/world-asia-china-28641008.

Greil, Arthur L. 1996. "Sacred Claims: The 'Cult Controversy' as a Struggle over the Right to the Religious Label." In *The Issue of Authenticity in the Study of Religion*, edited by David G. Bromley and Lewis F. Carter, 47–63. Greenwich, CT: JAI Press.

Guo, Baosheng. 2014. "警惕以 '邪教'名义大规模迫害基督教" (Be Wary of Persecution on Christianity in the Name of the "Cults"). *HRIC (Human Rights in China) Biweekly* 133 (June 13–26). http://biweeklyarchive.hrichina.org/article/18374.html.

Haohao [pseud.]. 2017. "The Growth of an Obedient Girl—Christian Testimony." Walk in the Light, November 10. https://www.hearthymn.com/the-growth-of-an-obedient-girl-christian-testimony.html.

Harris, Marvin. 1983. *Cultural Anthropology*. New York: Harper & Row.

Heggie, Rachel. 2017. "Where the Sacred and the Virtual Collide: The Church of Almighty God and Online Religion." MA thesis, Western Washington University.

Home Office. 2017. "Asylum Decision L145517." February 24. Copy in the archives of Center for Studies on New Religions, Torino, Italy.

Huang, Jiayun, Zhang Jun, and Zhang Suwen, dirs. 2017. *Where Is My Home*. Seoul: Judgment Seat of Christ Film Studio. Accessed February 21, 2018. https://www.youtube.com/watch?v=moHa5xIOZ18&t=4000s.

Human Rights without Frontiers. 2018a. *Tortured to Death: The Persecution of The Church of Almighty God in China*. Brussels: Human Rights without Frontiers and *Bitter Winter*.

Human Rights without Frontiers. 2018b. "Universal Periodic Review of China. Submission: The Persecution of The Church of Almighty God and Its Members." Submission to the United Nations' Human Rights Council. Accessed December 1, 2018. https://uprdoc.ohchr.org/uprweb/downloadfile.aspx?filename=5620&file=EnglishTranslation.

Immigration and Refugee Board of Canada. 2013. "China: The Church of Almighty God, Also Known as 'Eastern Lightning,' Including Its History, Beliefs, and Where It Is Present; Treatment of Members by Government Authorities." March 11. http://irb-cisr.gc.ca/Eng/ResRec/RirRdi/Pages/index.aspx?doc=454436&pls=1.

Immigration and Refugee Board of Canada. 2014a. "China: Religious Texts Used by the Church of the Almighty God (Eastern Lightning)." October 14. http://irb-cisr.gc.ca/Eng/ResRec/RirRdi/Pages/index.aspx?doc=455556&pls=1.

Immigration and Refugee Board of Canada. 2014b. "China: The Church of Almighty God (*Quannengshen*), Also Known as 'Eastern Lightning,' Including Its Leaders, Location and Activities Attributed to It: Treatment of Members by Authorities (March 2013–September 2014)." October 16. http://www.refworld.org/docid/546492804.html.

Introvigne, Massimo. 2011. "El hecho de la conversión religiosa." In *Conversión cristiana y evangelización*, edited by Juan Alonso and Juan José Alviar, 21–40. Pamplona: EUNSA.

Introvigne, Massimo. 2014. "Advocacy, Brainwashing Theories, and New Religious Movements." *Religion* 44(2): 303–19.

Introvigne, Massimo. 2017a. "Church of Almighty God." *Profiles of Millenarian & Apocalyptic Movements*, Center for the Critical Study of Apocalyptic and Millenarian Movements. Accessed February 6, 2018. https://censamm.org/resources/profiles/church-of-almighty-god.

Introvigne, Massimo. 2017b. "The Church of Almighty God and the Visual Arts." *World Religions and Spirituality Project*, December 3. https://wrldrels.org/2017/12/04/church-of-almighty-god-eastern-lightning-and-the-visual-arts/.

Introvigne, Massimo. 2017c. "'Cruel Killing, Brutal Killing, Kill the Beast': Investigating the 2014 McDonald's 'Cult Murder' in Zhaoyuan." *Journal of CESNUR* 1(1):61–73. doi:10.26338/tjoc.2017.1.1.6.

Introvigne, Massimo. 2017d. "Religious and Spiritual Movements and the Visual Arts: An Overview." *World Religions and Spirituality Project*, October 17. https://wrldrels.org/2017/10/19/religious-and-spiritual-movements-and-the-visual-arts/.

Introvigne, Massimo. 2018a. "Captivity Narratives: Did The Church of Almighty God Kidnap 34 Evangelical Pastors in 2002?" *Journal of CESNUR* 2(1):100–110. doi:10.26338/tjoc.2018.2.1.6.

Introvigne, Massimo. 2018b. "The Church of Almighty God: Is It a Religion? A Comment on the Order by the Court of Rome Dated January 19, 2018." *Journal of CESNUR* 2(1), supplement:45–48. doi:10.26338/tjoc.2018.supp.eng.2.1.

Introvigne, Massimo. 2018c. "Fake News! Chinese Mobilization of Resources against The Church of Almighty God as a Global Phenomenon." *Journal of CESNUR* 2(4):10–27. doi:10.26338/tjoc.2018.2.4.2.

Introvigne, Massimo. 2018d. "Family Networks and the Growth of The Church of Almighty God." *Interdisciplinary Journal of Research on Religion* 14(12):1–20. http://www.religjournal.com/pdf/ijrr14012.pdf.

Introvigne, Massimo. 2018e. "Gatekeeping and Narratives about 'Cult' Violence: The McDonald's Murder of 2014 in China." *Journal of Religion and Violence* 6(3):370–87. doi:10.5840/jrv20191960.

Introvigne, Massimo, dir. 2018f. *The Korean Hoax: False Demonstrations against Chinese Refugees in Seoul, Korea*. Documentary video Turin: Bitter Winter. Accessed January 10, 2019. https://youtu.be/nWOZlO87EK8.

Introvigne, Massimo. 2018g. *The Plymouth Brethren*. New York: Oxford University Press.

Introvigne, Massimo. 2018h. "Religious Freedom Problems in Russia and Hungary: A Case Study of the Church of Scientology." Paper presented at the conference Religious Freedom: Its Confirmation and Violation during the 20th and 21st Centuries, University of Eastern Finland, Joensuu, February 22–24.

Introvigne, Massimo, and David Bromley. 2017. "The Lü Yingchun/Zhang Fan Group." *World Religions and Spirituality Project*, October 16. https://wrldrels.org/2017/10/16/lu-yingchun-zhang-fan-group/.

Introvigne, Massimo, James T. Richardson, and Rosita Šorytė. 2019. "Would the Real Artticle 300 Please Stand Up? Refugees from Religious Movements Persecuted as *Xie Jiao* in China: The Case of The Church of Almighty God." *Journal of CESNUR* 3(5):3–86. doi 10.26338/tjoc.2019.3.5.1.

Irons, Edward. 2018. "The List: The Evolution of China's List of Illegal and Evil Cults." *Journal of CESNUR* 2(1):33–57. doi:10.26338/tjoc.2018.2.1.3.

Irons, Edward. 2019. "Major Changes in the Structures for Fighting Xie Jiao in China." *Bitter Winter*, February 24. https://bitterwinter.org/changes-in-the-structures-for-fighting-xie-jiao/.

Jeju Ilbo. 2017. "中 전능신교 신도 제주로 유입 . . . 난민신청 쇄도." (The Church of Almighty God Believers Swarming into Jeju to Seek Refugee Status.) October 30. http://www.jejuilbo.net/news/articleView.html?idxno=65496.

Kaiwind Net. 2016. "山东招远麦当劳杀人案行凶者的狱中忏悔" (Confessions of Remorse by the Imprisoned Murderers of the McDonald's Murder in Zhaoyuan, Shandong). May 28. http://anticult.kaiwind.com/xingao/2016/201605/28/t20160528_3879217.shtml.

Kilbourne, Brock K., and James T. Richardson. 1984. "Psychotherapy and New Religions in a Pluralistic Society." *American Psychologist* 39(3):237–51. doi:10.1037/0003-066X.39.3.237.

Kilbourne, Brock K., and James T. Richardson. 1986. "Cultphobia." *Thought: Fordham University Quarterly* 61(2):258–66. doi:10.5840/thought19866126.

KKNews. 2017."反邪動態」美國、義大利專家赴鄭州進行反邪教學術交流" ("Anti-Cult": US, Italian Experts Went to Zhengzhou for Anti-Cult Academic Exchanges). July 11. https://kknews.cc/society/rrr2m8o.html.

Lam, Nuala Gathercole. 2017. "Police Arrest Disciples of Chinese Female Jesus." *Sixth Tone*, July 26. http://www.sixthtone.com/news/1000581/police-arrest-disciples-of-chinese-female-jesus.

Lamb, Christopher, and M. Darroll Bryant, eds. 1999. *Religious Conversion: Contemporary Practices and Controversies*. London: Cassell.

Levy, Neil. 2017. "The Bad News about Fake News." *Social Epistemology Review and Reply Collective* 6(8):20–36. https://social-epistemology.com/2017/07/24/the-bad-news-about-fake-news-neil-levy/.

Li, Jianglin. 2016. *Tibet in Agony: Lhasa 1959*. Cambridge, MA: Harvard University Press.

Li, Jie. 2018. "Affidavit." June 18. Copy in the archives of CESNUR, Torino, Italy.

Li, Yuan. 2017. "At the Congress Xi Reaffirms: Sinicization of Religions under the Communist Party." *AsiaNews*, October 19. http://www.asianews.it/news-en/At-the-Congress-Xi-Reaffirms:-Sinicization-of-religions-under-the-Communist-Party-42096.html.

Ling, Liu. 2015. "Female-Christ Warriors: A Study of the Church of Almighty God." *Cultural Diversity in China* 1(2):233–49.

Ma, Xingrui. 2014. "马兴瑞同志在省委防范和处理邪教问题领导小组全体成员会议上的讲话" (Comrade Ma Xingrui's Talk on the Meeting Open to All Members of the Provincial 610 Office). Association for the Protection of Human Rights and Religious Freedom. Accessed December 21, 2017. https://www.adhrrf.org/china-ma-xingrui-20140709.html.

MacFarquhar, Roderick, and Michael Schoenhals. 2006. *Mao's Last Revolution*. Cambridge, MA: Belknap Press of Harvard University Press.

Max. 2018. "I Will No Longer Define the Gender of the Returned Lord by My Imagination." Find a Shepherd, July 17. https://www.findshepherd.com/no-longer-define.html.

Melton, J. Gordon. 2018. "Xiejiao, Cults, and New Religions: Making Sense of the New Un-Sinicized Religions on China's Fringe." Paper presented at the conference Sinicization of Religion in China: From Above and Below. University of California, San Diego, March 22.

Meng, Yuanxin. 2018. "The New Socialism Reform or Delusion to Eradicate Religion: An Analysis of the New Religious Affairs Regulations and the Chinese Communist Party's Religious Policy during the Xi Administration." *Chinese Law and Religion Monitor* 11(1):21–64.

Miller, Claire Cain. 2014. "The iPad as a Canvas." *New York Times*, January 13, B5.

Mintz, Zoe. 2014. "China's Cult Crackdown: What Is The Church of Almighty God?" *International Business Times*, December 10. http://www.ibtimes.com/chinas-cult-crackdown-what-church-almighty-god-1747990.

Ministerio de Justicia. 2016. "Detalle de entidades religiosas: Iglesia de Dios Todopoderoso." Accessed March 29, 2019. https://maper.mjusticia.gob.es/Maper/DetalleEntidadReligiosa.action?numeroInscripcion=023139.

Moore, Malcolm. 2015. "Inside China's Most Radical Cult." *The Telegraph*, February 2. https://www.telegraph.co.uk/news/worldnews/asia/china/11046155/Inside-Chinas-most-radical-cult.html.

Nancy. 2014. "Six People Killed the Woman in McDonald's, May 28th, China." *CNN iReport*, June 1. http://ireport.cnn.com/docs/DOC-1139281 No longer available.

Omnium des Libertés and Canaan Human Rights. 2018. "Universal Periodic Review, China. Religious Persecution in China: The Case of The Church of Almighty God." Submission to the United Nations' Human Rights Council. Accessed December 1, 2018. https://uprdoc.ohchr.org/uprweb/downloadfile.aspx?filename=5586&file=EnglishTranslation.

Palmer, David Alexander. 2012. "Heretical Doctrines, Reactionary Secret Societies, Evil Cults: Labelling Heterodoxy in 20th-Century China." In *Chinese Religiosities: The Vicissitudes of Modernity and State Formation*, edited by Mayfair Yang, 113–34. Berkeley: University of California Press.

Pan, Junliang. 2015. "Messianism and Politics in Contemporary China: The Church of Almighty God." *Review of Religion and Chinese Society* 2:186–215.

Panpan [pseud.]. 2017. "A Post-90s Couple's Secret of Togetherness." Walk in the Light, September 14. https://www.hearthymn.com/a-post-90s-couples-secret-of-togetherness.html.

People's Daily. 2014. "Inside China's 'Eastern Lightning' Cult." June 3. http://en.people.cn/n/2014/0603/c90882-8735801.html.

Permanent Mission of the People's Republic of China to the United Nations and Other International Organizations in Vienna. N.d. "Criminal Law of the People's Republic of China." Accessed April 11, 2018. http://www.fmprc.gov.cn/ce/cgvienna/eng/dbtyw/jdwt/crimelaw/t209043.htm.

Phoenix Satellite TV. 2014. "社会能见度 审判"全能神" (Social Watch: Trial on Almighty God). August 21. https://web.archive.org/web/20181209110109/http:/ucwap.ifeng.com/client/channelone/fenghuang/news?aid=88221898&rt=1&mid=1544315213461_ap596v5404&p=1.

Pike, Sarah. 2009. "Dark Teens and Born-Again Martyrs: Captivity Narratives after Columbine." *Journal of the American Academy of Religion* 77(3):647–79. doi:10.1093/jaarel/lfp038.

Pingtan County. 2015. "关于对邪教组织非法传播活动实行举报奖励制度的通知" (Notice on Enforcing Regulations of Rewarding Informers against the Unlawful Circulation Activities of *Xie Jiao*). Accessed April 11, 2018. http://www.pingtan.gov.cn/site/main/info/gov_ml_show.jsp?documentid=9202.

Qimiao [pseud.]. 2017. "Who Can Reconcile the Relation between Mother-in-Law and Daughter-in-Law?" Walk in the Light, November 3. https://www.hearthymn.com/gods-word-can-reconcile-the-relation.html.

Reny, Marie-Ève. 2018. *Authoritarian Containment: Public Security Bureaus and Protestant House Churches in Suburban China*. New York: Oxford University Press.

Richardson, James T. 1978. "An Oppositional and General Conceptualization of Cult." *Annual Review of the Social Sciences of Religion* 2:29–52.

Richardson, James T. 1979. "From Cult to Sect: Creative Eclecticism in New Religious Movements." *Pacific Sociological Review* 22(2):139–66. doi:10.2307/1388875.

Richardson, James T. 1993. "Definitions of Cult: From Sociological-Technical to Popular-Negative." *Review of Religious Research* 34(4):348–56. doi:10.2307/3511972.

Richardson, James T. 1996. "Sociology and the New Religions: 'Brainwashing,' the Courts, and Religious Freedom." In *Witnessing for Sociology: Sociologists in Court*, edited by Pamela Jenkins and Steve Kroll-Smith, 115–37. Westport, CT: Praeger.

Rini, Regina. 2017. "Fake News and Partisan Epistemology." *Kennedy Institute of Ethics Journal* 27(2):E43–E64. doi:10.1353/ken.2017.0025.

Robbins, Thomas. 1988. *Cults, Converts and Charisma: The Sociology of New Religious Movements*. London: Sage.

Rongsheng, Bi. 2001. "石家庄市公安局一处关於转发河北省公安厅宗教处毕荣生副处长在'807'专案协调会上的讲话的通知" (The First Division of Shijiazhuang Public Security Bureau: Notice on Forwarding the [September 14, 2000] Speech of Bi Rongsheng, Deputy Director of the Religion Section of Public Security Department of Hebei Province, on the "807" Case Coordination Meeting). October 9. https://www.adhrrf.org/wp-content/grand-media/application/_-_807_.pdf.

Runhua, Zhao. 2018. "Qinghai Police Announce Success against Cult." *Caixin Global News*, December 28. https://www.caixinglobal.com/2018-12-28/qinghai-police-announce-success-against-cult-101364654.html.

Shandong Anti-Cult Association. 2017. "临沂市出台《群众举报邪教组织违法犯罪线索奖励办法" (Resolution to Rewarding Citizens Providing Clues about Xie Jiao Crimes Issued by Linyi City). May 8. https://web.archive.org/web/20171115104441/http:/www.sdfxj.org/dxal/201705/08/t20170508_5176711.shtml.

Shao, Yong. 1997. 中國會道門 (Chinese Sects and Secret Societies). Shanghai: Shanghai renmin chubanshe.

Shen, Xiaoming, and Eugene Bach. 2017. *Kidnapped by a Cult: A Pastor's Stand against a Murderous Sect*. New Kensington, PA: Whitaker House.

Snow, David A., Louis A. Zurcher Jr., and Sheldon R. Ekland-Olson. 1980. "Social Networks and Social Movements: A Microstructural Approach to Differential Recruitment." *American Sociological Review* 45(5):787–801. doi:10.2307/2094895.

Snow, David A., Louis A. Zurcher Jr., and Sheldon R. Ekland-Olson. 1983. "Further Thoughts on Social Networks and Movement Recruitment." *Sociology* 17(1):112–20. doi:10.1177/0038038583017001008.

Šorytė, Rosita. 2018. "Religious Persecution, Refugees, and Right of Asylum: The Case of The Church of Almighty God." *Journal of CESNUR* 2(1):78–99. doi:10.26338/tjoc.2018.2.1.5.

Soteria International and Association on Study of Religion and Human Rights. 2018. "Universal Periodic Review, China. Submission: Religious Freedom in China, A Cause of Concern." Submission to the United Nations' Human Rights Council. Accessed December 1, 2018. https://uprdoc.ohchr.org/uprweb/downloadfile.aspx?filename=5706&file=EnglishTranslation.

Stark, Rodney, and Roger Finke. 2000. *Acts of Faith: Explaining the Human Side of Religion*. Berkeley: University of California Press.

Stark, Rodney, and Lynne Roberts. 1982. "The Arithmetic of Social Movements." *Sociological Analysis* 43(1):53–68. doi:10.2307/3711418.

Supreme People's Procuratorate of the People's Republic of China. 2017. "关于办理组织、利用邪教组织破坏法律实施等刑事案件适用法律若干问题的解释" (Interpretations on the Issues concerning the Application of Laws in Criminal Cases relating to Organizing and Utilizing Evil Organizations to Destroy Law Enforcement). January 25. http://www.spp.gov.cn/zdgz/201701/t20170126_179794.shtml.

Ta Kung Pao. 2017. "深度調查|邪教'全能神'蠱惑新移民婦再煽末日" (In-depth Investigation on Xie Jiao 'Almighty God' Inciting New Female Immigrants to Proclaim Again the Doomsday). November 20. http://news.takungpao.com.hk/hkol/topnews/2017-11/3516795.html.

Tan, Chee-Beng, ed. 2012. *Routledge Handbook of the Chinese Diaspora*. London: Routledge.

ter Haar, Baarend J. 1992. *The White Lotus Teachings in Chinese Religious History*. Leiden: Brill.

United Nations High Commissioner for Refugees. 2004. *Guidelines on International Protection: Religion-Based Refugee Claims under Article 1A(2) of the 1951 Convention and/or the 1967 Protocol relating to the Status of Refugees*. Geneva: UNHCR. Accessed April 29, 2018. http://www.unhcr.org/publications/legal/40d8427a4/guidelines-international-protection-6-religion-based-refugee-claims-under.html.

United Nations Human Rights Council. 2018. "Summary of Stakeholders' Submissions on China: Report of the Office of the United Nations High Commissioner for Human Rights." Accessed January 29, 2019. https://

documents-dds-ny.un.org/doc/UNDOC/GEN/G18/266/48/PDF/G1826648.pdf?OpenElement.
United States Commission on International Religious Freedom). 2019. *2019 Annual Report.* Washington D.C.: United States Commission on International Religious Freedom.
U.S. Congress, Tom Lantos Human Rights Commission. 2019. "Mo Xiufeng." January 29. https://humanrightscommission.house.gov/defending-freedom-project/prisoners-by-country/China/Mo%20Xiufeng.
U.S. Department of State. 2014. *Country Reports on Human Right Practices—China.* Accessed April 11, 2018. http://www.state.gov/j/drl/rls/hrrpt/humanrightsreport/index.htm?year=2014&dlid=236432.
U.S. Department of State. 2019a. *Country Reports on Human Rights Practices—China.* Accessed March 29, 2019. https://www.state.gov/documents/organization/289281.pdf.
U.S. Department of State. 2019b. *International Religious Freedom Report 2018—China (Includes Tibet, Xinjiang, Hong Kong, and Macau).* Accessed September 9, 2019. https://www.state.gov/wp-content/uploads/2019/05/CHINA-INCLUSIVE-2018-INTERNATIONAL-RELIGIOUS-FREEDOM-REPORT.pdf.
Vala, Carsten T. 2018. *The Politics of Protestant Churches and the Party-State in China: God above Party?* London: Routledge.
Wang, Duruo. 2014. "内部消息：麦当劳内打死美女暴徒 是公安局长孙宝东帮凶" (Inside News: Violent Murderer Responsible for the Beauty's Death at McDonald's. Declarations by Sun Baodong, the Chief Head of Public Security Bureau). *Aboluowang,* June 1. http://www.aboluowang.com/2014/0601/402013.html.
Wen Wei Po. 2017. "邪教攻港 「全能神」蛊惑新移民妇再煽末日" (Xie Jiao Attacking HK—"Almighty God" Inciting New Female Immigrants to Proclaim Again the Doomsday). Accessed April 27, 2018. http://news.wenweipo.com/2017/11/20/IN1711200009.htm.
Whitaker House. 2017. "Eugene Bach: Kidnapped by a Cult." YouTube, February 7. https://www.youtube.com/watch?v=OqI5jyy7Evc.
Xia, Ding. 2017. "God Is in Charge of My Family." Find a Shepherd, September 11. https://www.findshepherd.com/god-is-in-charge-of-my-family.html.
Xiao, Hui, and Zhang Yongsheng, with Han Xuefeng, Zhong Yuhao, and Sun Beibe. 2014. "一个'全能神教'家庭的发展史" (History of the Family of "The Group of Almighty God"). *Beijing News,* August 22. http://www.bjnews.com.cn/inside/2014/08/22/330806.html.
Xiaolin [pseud.]. 2016. "Almighty God's Word Leads Me to Associate Normally with Others." Find a Shepherd, January 18. https://www.findshepherd.com/almighty-gods-word-leads-me.html.

Xie Qiang. 2015. "I Have Received Almighty God's Great Salvation." Gospel of the Descent of the Kingdom, August 19. https://www.holyspiritspeaks.org/19-i-have-received-almighty-gods-great-salvation.

Xin, Shuyan. 2014. "辛树言：中国当局何曾尊重过宗教信仰自由" (The Chinese Authorities Never Respect Religious Freedom). *HRIC (Human Rights in China) Biweekly* 134 (June 27–July 10). http://www.hrichina.org/chs/zhong-guo-ren-quan-shuang-zhou-kan/xin-shu-yan-zhong-guo-dang-ju-he-ceng-zun-zhong-guo-zong-jia.

Xinhua. 2017. "18 Detained in Connection to Cult Activities." July 26. http://www.xinhuanet.com/english/2017-07/26/c_136474914.htm.

Xu, Tao. 2017. "The Comparison and Dialogue of Definitions of Cult between China and America." Paper presented at the conference The Question of Xiejiao in China and the Case of the Church of Almighty God, University of Hong Kong, September 15–16. Manuscript in the conference booklet.

Yang, Fenggang. 2004. "Between Secularist Ideology and Desecularizing Reality: The Birth and Growth of Religious Research in Communist China." *Sociology of Religion* 65(2):101–19.

Yang, Fenggang. 2006. "The Red, Black, and Gray Markets of Religion in China." *Sociological Quarterly* 47(1):93–122. doi:10.1111/j.1533-8525.2006.00039.x.

Yang, Fenggang. 2012. *Religion in China: Survival and Revival under Communist Rule.* New York: Oxford University Press.

Zheng, Yi, and Li Mo, dirs. 2017. *Child, Come Back Home.* Seoul: Judgment Seat of Christ Film Studio. Accessed February 21, 2018. https://www.youtube.com/watch?v=qF4L4wcYv_w.

Zhien [pseud.]. 2017. "I Finally 'Regained' My Lovely Son." Find a Shepherd, August 27. https://www.findshepherd.com/i-finally-regained-my-lovely-son.html.

Zoccatelli, PierLuigi. 2018. "Anti-Cult Campaigns in China and the Case of The Church of Almighty God: An Introduction." *Journal of CESNUR* 2(1):3–12. doi: 10.26338/tjoc.2018.2.1.1.

Zoccatelli, PierLuigi. 2019. "宣誓供述書" (Affidavit). *Journal of CESNUR* 3(2):81–86. doi:10.26338/tjoc.2019.3.2.8.

Index of Personal Names

Adam, 43, 76, 94
Ai, Yan-Ling, 106
Aikman, David, 130, 133
Allen-Ebrahimian, Bethany, 103, 133
Alonso, Juan, 139
Alviar, Juan José, 139
Ann (CAG member), 51, 52, 133
Anthony, Dick, 24, 133

Bach, Eugene, 106, 111, 143, 145
Bai, Shuangfeng, 6
Barker, Eileen, 55, 133
Bright, Steve, 109, 134
Bromley, David G., 93, 112, 133, 138, 140
Bryant, M. Darroll, 55, 141

Calvani, Cristina, 125, 134
Carter, Lewis F. (1940–2019), 138
Chan, Kim-kwong, 114, 134
Chan, Lois, 109, 134
Charlie (CAG member), 53, 54, 67
Chen, Lin, 5
Chen, Lu, 88, 134
Chen, Qingping, 23–25, 134
Chen, Wei, 61, 135
Chen, Xiujuan, 90, 94, 95
Cheng, Xin, 33
Ching Hai, 20
Chiniquy, Charles P. (1809–1899), 25
Christopher (pseudonym, CAG member), 54, 55, 135
Ciotta, Luca, xi
Connor, Neil, 103, 137
Cui, Shuya, 12, 13

Danny (CAG member), 51
Davis, David Brion (1927–2019), 25, 81, 137

Deng, Xiaoping (1904–1997), 28, 128–131
Dunn, Emily, 27, 29, 38, 42, 43, 47, 70, 72, 83–86, 88–90, 105, 106, 109–112, 115, 137

Ekland-Olson, Sheldon R., 55, 144
Elliott, Mark C., 16, 138
Eve, 43, 76, 94

Fan, Bin, 91, 92
Fan, Longfeng, 91, 92
Fang, Yuwei, 83, 138
Finke, Roger, 49, 50, 144
Flinchbaugh, C. Hope, 106, 138
Flora (Sister), 51
Folk, Holly, x, xi, 44, 72, 73, 84, 85, 102, 138

Gallagher, Eugene V., 25, 81, 138
Gao, Cuiqin (1963–2014), 7–9
Gelfert, Axel, 80, 138
Gong, Yuebing, 7
Goossaert, Vincent, 19, 138
Gracie, Carrie, 56, 82, 138
Greil, Arthur Larry, 25, 138
Guo, Baosheng, 99, 138
Guo, Bin, 85

Han, Xuefeng, 145
Haohao (pseudonym, CAG member), 60, 138
Harris, Marvin, 49, 138
He, Linbo, 13–15
He, Zhexun, 40
Heggie, Rachel, 68, 138
Hockney, David, 76
Huang, Jiayun, 61, 138
Hunt, William Holman (1827–1910), 77

148 INDEX OF PERSONAL NAMES

Introvigne, Massimo, 21, 24, 25, 28, 55, 56, 61, 70, 75, 76, 78, 80, 81, 83, 93, 100, 102, 119, 120, 133, 139, 140
Irons, Edward, xi, 19, 20, 22, 140

Jenkins, Pamela, 143
Jesus Christ, ix, x, 24, 27–30, 36, 39, 41–44, 48, 50, 52, 54, 56, 58, 68, 73, 77, 78, 90, 133, 137, 141
Ji, Sanbao (1940–1997), 90
Jia (Brother), 106
Jiang, Guizhi (1966–2013), vii, 4–7
Jiao, Fuqun, 9, 10
Jing (Brother), 108

Kilbourne, Brock K., 55, 141
Kroll-Smith, Steve, 143

Lam, Nuala Gathercole, 103, 141
Lamb, Christopher, 55, 141
Lao-Tzu (ca. 6th century BCE), 131
Lee, Witness (1905–1997), 28
Levy, Neil, 80, 141
Li, Changshou. *See* Lee, Witness
Li, Jianglin, 127, 141
Li, Jie, 7, 141
Li, Mo, 61, 146
Li, Shu-Xia (Sister), 106
Li, Youwang, 91, 92
Li, Yuan, 17, 18, 141
Li, Zhenyuan, 121, 122
Lian (Brother), 106, 107, 109
Lin, Bo-en, 77
Ling, Liu, 70, 141
Liu, Limei (1970–2014), 1, 2
Liu, Mr., 8
Lü, Yingchun, 90–101, 140

Ma, Suoping (1969–2009), 40
Ma, Xingrui, 41, 49, 121, 141
MacFarquhar, Roderick (1930–2019), 127, 141
Mao, Zedong (1893–1976), 19, 126–129, 141
Max (CAG member), 52, 53, 141
Melton, J. Gordon, xi, 23, 25, 84, 141

Meng, Yuanxin, 128, 141
Miller, Claire Cain, 76, 142
Mintz, Zoe, 87, 88, 142
Mo, Xiufeng, viii, 145
Moore, Malcolm, 82, 142
Moses (Prophet), 37

Nan, Xiangming (1942–2016), 9–11
"Nancy" (pseudonym), 98, 142
Nee, Watchman (1903–1972), 28
Ni Shu-Tsu. *See* Nee, Watchman
Noah, 56, 77

O, Myung-Ok, 104, 119

Palmer, David Alexander, 19, 24, 138, 142
Palmer, Susan, xi
Pan, Junliang, 70, 92, 142
Panpan (pseudonym, CAG member), 60, 142
Peter (Apostle), 37, 77
Pike, Sarah, 112, 142
Pokorny, Lukas, 137
Putin, Vladimir, 81

Qi (Brother), 108
Qimiao (pseudonym, CAG member), 143

Reny, Marie-Ève, 18, 143
Richardson, James T., xi, 21, 25, 55, 81, 120, 140, 141, 143
Rigal-Cellard, Bernadette, xi
Rini, Regina, 80, 143
Robbins, Thomas (1943–2015), 55, 143
Roberts, Lynne, 55, 144
Rongsheng, Bi, 39, 143
Runhua, Zhao, 120, 143

Schoenhals, Michael, 127, 141
Shao, Yong, 19, 143
Shen, Xiaoming, 106, 107, 109, 111, 143
Shen, Yiping, 109
Snow, David A., 55, 144
Šorytė, Rosita, xi, 21, 117, 120, 140, 144
Stark, Rodney, 49, 50, 55, 144
Sun, Baodong, 145

Sun, Beibe, 145
Sun, Teng, 135

Tan, Chee-Beng, 123, 144
ter Haar, Baarend J., 19, 144
Tian, Mrs., 117, 118
Tina (CAG member), 53, 54, 67

Ulpianus (170–223), 26

Vala, Carsten T., 18, 130, 131, 145

Wang, Duruo, 90, 145
Wang, Xiumei, 122, 123, 135
Wei (Brother), 109
Winter, Franz, 137
Wu, Shuoyan (1977–2014), 88, 96, 97
Wu, Tong, 61, 135

Xi, Jinping, 17, 126, 128–130, 132, 141
Xia, Ding, 60, 145
Xiao, Hui, 91, 92, 95, 145
Xiaolin (pseudonym, CAG member), 60, 145
Xie, Guangsheng, 135
Xie, Qiang, 110, 111, 113, 146
Xin, Rui, 33
Xin, Shuyan, 99, 146
Xing (Brother), 108
Xing, Dao, 33
Xu, Tao, 23, 24, 146
Xue, Mingxue. *See* Xie, Qiang

Yang (Brother), 106–108
Yang, Feng, 133

Yang, Fenggang, 18, 126, 128, 146
Yang, Mayfair, 142
Yang, Shihua, 122
Yang, Xiangbin, 29
Yin, Junxiu, 61, 135
Yu, Edward, 107
Yu, Hongchao, 4

Zhang (Brother), 108
Zhang, Delan, 135
Zhang, Duo, 90, 94, 98
Zhang, Fan (1984–2015), 90–101, 140
Zhang, Fu, 117, 118
Zhang, Hang, 90, 96–98, 100, 101
Zhang, Jun, 61, 138
Zhang, Li, 4
Zhang, Lidong (1959–2015), 88, 90, 94–99
Zhang, Qiaolian, 90, 93, 94, 98
Zhang, Ruixia (1961–2015), 11, 12
Zhang, Suwen, 61, 138
Zhang, Yongsheng, 91, 92, 95, 145
Zhao (Sister), 108
Zhao, Weishan, 29, 30, 37, 39, 58–60, 71, 85, 86, 93, 115
Zhao, Xuepeng, 8
Zheng, Ms., 4
Zheng, Yang, 3
Zheng, Yi, 61, 146
"Zhien" (pseudonym, CAG member), 60, 146
Zhong, Yuhao, 145
Zoccatelli, PierLuigi, 23, 123, 146
Zurcher, Louis. A., Jr. (1936–1987), 55, 144